OUTSMART ARTHRITIS

Prevention is a registered trademark of Rodale Inc.
This edition first published in the UK in 2004 by Rodale Ltd, 7-10 Chandos Street, London W1G 9AD (0207 291 6000).
Printed and bound in the UK by Southernprint.
Colour separation by Graphics Kent.
ISSN 1478-4998

WWW.RODALESTORE.CO.UK

EDITOR: Steven Seaton

ART DIRECTOR: Russell Fairbrother

SUB-EDITOR: Karen Tigar

STAFF WRITER: Marguerite Lazell

PHOTO RESEARCH: Rupert Elkington-Cole

EDITORIAL ASSISTANT: Tom Phillips

CONTRIBUTING EDITORS: Rick Chillot, Patricia deSa, Julie Evans, Sherry Weiss Kiser, Barbara Loecher, Holly McCord, Miriam Nelson, Linda Rao, Denise Barrett, Sarah Roberton, Rob Spedding, Denise Webb

UK Production

PRODUCTION DIRECTOR: Matthew Jolly

PRODUCTION MANAGER: Andy Parslow

AD PRODUCTION MANAGER: Nicky Rouse

AD PRODUCTION ASSISTANT: Catherine Perry

UK Circulation

CIRCULATION DIRECTOR: Tim Moore

CIRCULATION OPERATIONS MANAGER: Helen Knight

CIRCULATION ANALYST: Emma Smyth

CIRCULATION MARKETING COORDINATOR: Aaron Gekoski

CIRCULATION ASSISTANT: Kate McGregor

Rodale Women's Health Group

PRESIDENT, WOMEN'S PUBLISHING GROUP: Sara Levinson

VICE PRESIDENT, EDITORIAL DIRECTOR: Rosemary Ellis

Prevention Special Interest Publications

EXECUTIVE EDITOR: Cindi Caciolo

RODALE

WE INSPIRE AND ENABLE PEOPLE TO IMPROVE THEIR LIVES AND THE WORLD AROUND THEM

4 CONTENTS

p17
Eat right to boost your immunity

PART **THREE**

strong nutrition for strong joints

What you eat can have a positive—or negative—effect on your arthritis

p45
Surgery can give you a new lease of life

p62
Place the emphasis on fruit and veg when you shop

p106
Walk away the
pain

p142
**Don't let arthritis
control your life**

PART **SIX**

the arthritis action plan
**The best way to take on arthritis is one day at
a time**

p150
**30 days to a
healthier you**

You Can't Cure it But You Can Control it

Over seven million adults in the UK are estimated to suffer from arthritis. One in five visits to a GP are related to arthritis. Over 200 million working days a year are lost because of arthritis.

There is no question that arthritis, in its many forms, is one of the country's biggest health issues. Yet, perhaps because it debilitates and disables rather than kills, it doesn't receive the attention it deserves.

That's why we've put together this special book. It combines the knowledge and expertise of *Prevention* magazine—the world's biggest and most successful health title—with information from some of Britain's leading experts to provide a comprehensive arthritis guide you can trust.

There is currently no cure for arthritis, although you can treat the symptoms of the condition with a range of conventional and alternative therapies (see pages 40-59). But that isn't the only route. We now know that you can do far more to fight back against arthritis and take control of your life again. Here are just a few of the tips you'll find inside:

➤ Eating the right foods can help reduce joint inflammation and tenderness. See pages 62-73 to discover which foods you should be eating—and which you should avoid—for optimum relief.
➤ Walking literally cleanses and feeds your joints with every step to relieve arthritis symptoms. See page 108 for a simple programme that really works.
➤ Taking glucosamine has been proven to rebuild cartilage and slow the progression of osteoarthritis. Find out which other supplements could help your condition on pages 74-79.

Throughout this volume there are hundreds of other nuggets of useful information. That information is a powerful weapon in the fight against arthritis. The better informed you are, the more able you are to deal with your condition and the restrictions that it can impose on you. We hope that this book will provide you with much of the information you need to outsmart arthritis both today and into the future.

Steven Seaton
Editor

SUBSCRIBE TO Men'sHealth

THE WORLD'S BEST SELLING MEN'S LIFESTYLE MAGAZINE

SAVE 30%
ON THE NORMAL ANNUAL SUBSCRIPTION PRICE

Delivery direct to your door each month

Access to free online articles and downloads - only available to subscribers

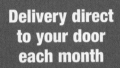

Every issue will show you how to live healthier, look better, be stronger and live longer. Plus tons of useful tips to help you be smarter about life's choices including:

▶ **Health & Fitness:** Tips to help you ease yourself into a healthier lifestyle

▶ **Wealth:** Tips to help you get smarter with your finances

▶ **Nutrition:** Tips to help you discover hundreds of energy boosting foods that improve performance at work, home and play

▶ **Stress:** Tips on how to identify and beat stress as well as combat fatigue

▶ **Grooming:** Tips to help you look better with minimum effort

Subscribe to Men's Health for one year (11 issues) for only £27.97, saving over 30% off the normal annual subscription price. All subscribers will not only receive Men's Health delivered direct to their door every issue, but will also receive access to online content, only available to subscribers.

Please call **01858 438851** quoting code 1566

arthritis explained

From what it is to how it's treated, everything you need to know about this disease

CHAPTER 1

Take Control of Osteoarthritis

Learn whether you're at risk—and what to do if you are

Osteoarthritis (OA) isn't supposed to happen to people in their 30s. But don't tell that to Diane Hopwood. When she was 39, Hopwood was diagnosed with OA of the spine, knees, hands, and ankles. Now 47, she's had surgery on her back, her ankle, and one knee, and she expects to need surgery on her other knee. It's just a matter of time, she says.

As an exercise physiologist who has been helping others with OA for nearly 20 years, Hopwood should have recognized the warning signs—in her case, stiffness and pain during and after exercise, combined with a strong family history of arthritis.

50 per cent of sufferers are under 65

But like many competitive athletes, she pushed herself to the limit, running on worn-out knees and lifting weights with a spine that simply wasn't prepared to handle the amount of stress she placed on it.

And that may have worsened the condition, she concedes. "Had I paid attention to my body and known what was going on, I may have been able to avoid surgery by doing the proper types of exercise for someone with my condition," she says.

She is eager that others learn from her experience. Among her lessons is this nugget of wisdom: Don't think that OA strikes only the 65-plus crowd.

"I've seen a lot of people in their late 20s and early 30s with arthritis," says Hopwood. In fact, as many as half of the more than two million Britons affected by OA are under 65. But there's no need to panic. In the following pages, we'll tell you how to assess your risk—but it's important to take action now. Early and accurate diagnosis is critical to keep this disease from preventing you from doing what you love.

What exactly is osteoarthritis?

Of more than 100 types of arthritis, OA is the most common: two million people in the UK are being treated for the condition. Many more are undiagnosed—in fact, the Arthritis Research Campaign estimates that 7 million people suffer from some form of arthritis.

Osteoarthritis is a joint disease that mostly affects cartilage, the slippery tissue that covers and protects the ends of your bones in the joint.

When cartilage breaks down, as it does in people with osteoarthritis, bone may rub on bone, causing pain and swelling, and restricting motion. No one knows exactly why cartilage deteriorates, although genetics, anatomical structure problems, and injury all play a role.

Who's at risk?

Osteoarthritis typically affects people over 40 and your risk increases as you age. Almost 80 per cent of people over the age of 50 show signs of osteoarthritis-like joint damage and about a quarter of them feel pain. But it can happen sooner, especially if you've had a joint injury at some stage.

Being overweight can lead to OA because of the extra stress it puts on the joints. The recent rise in the incidence of obesity in the UK is one of the most regularly cited reasons for the corresponding rise in OA over the last decade. Family history can be a factor too: middle-aged and older women with a family history of OA have a particularly high risk of developing the disease. But while age is a factor, OA is not an inevitable part of ageing.

Early diagnosis pays off

You *can* nip osteoarthritis in the bud

How is OA diagnosed?

Your GP makes a diagnosis of OA based on a physical examination of your joints (a doctor should be able to feel the swelling and creaking of the joints and notice restricted movement or tenderness), combined with questions about your family (did your parents or grandparents have it?), past joint injuries, and any symptoms you've experienced. If you're overweight and physically inactive, your doctor will also take that into account.

Unfortunately, there aren't any tests to definitively diagnose OA. Your doctor may order blood or urine tests to rule out other sorts of arthritis, or they may send you to get an X-ray of the affected joint. X-rays tend to be more helpful in the later stages of OA, when there is loss of cartilage or changes to the bone.

How can my doctor help?

The first stages of OA may be silent; the mild cartilage damage typically has no symptoms. OA is most likely to show up in hands and weight-bearing joints, including the knees, hips, lower back, neck, and end joints of the fingers. But it's only when there is significant cartilage loss that you'll begin to notice real pain and loss of joint function. So once you feel those first twinges, you need to see your doctor to prevent further damage.

Many people assume that arthritis pain is just part of getting old, and that they're going to have to put up with it. But that's simply not

TAKE CONTROL

Discover Glucosamine

Once viewed as just another unproven treatment for OA, glucosamine may be the first treatment to actually slow the loss of cartilage that's the hallmark of the disease. In a Belgian study following 212 people with OA of the knee for 3 years, glucosamine not only relieved their pain, but also slowed destruction of the protective cartilage lining their knee joints.

true. A doctor can offer diagnosis, pain-relieving medication, and, most importantly, invaluable information about stopping OA from getting worse. If you don't take care of your OA now, you risk disability later on, and the possibility of joint replacement surgery. Not all joint pain is OA, but you need to see your GP to rule out other reasons.

Is OA preventable?

Yes, and as there is no cure for OA, prevention is your best bet. You can lower your risk by being active, stretching before exercise (see Chapter 11), staying at a healthy weight, and preventing joint injuries. We tend to think of a healthy heart as the main reason to keep fit and keep our weight down, but preventing OA is another good reason.

Weight loss can help if you already suffer from OA, and you don't have to lose a lot to make a difference. When you walk, your knees absorb a force equal to approximately three times your bodyweight with each step. So for every pound you lose on every stride, there is three pounds less load on your knees.

I have OA, what's next?

If you're in pain, your doctor will recommend over-the-counter or prescription painkillers. Along with dietary changes to lose weight (if necessary), they should also suggest you take up aerobic activity and perform exercises to strengthen the muscles around the joints.

Won't exercise hurt?

If you want to feel less pain, take fewer

High-risk factors

➤ **Age** The older you get, the higher your risk of OA. Those in their 60s are far more likely to be affected than those under 40.

➤ **Gender** There is a far greater incidence of OA in women than men.

➤ **Weight** Being overweight or obese is the single biggest preventable risk factor for OA, especially of the knee. It will also worsen the condition once it's developed.

➤ **History** Some forms of OA—in the hands—have an hereditary link.

➤ **Injury** A major trauma injury to a joint can often develop into OA at the same site later in life.

medications, improve your flexibility, get stronger, and avoid joint replacement surgery in the future, you have to get moving. Some studies show that aerobic exercise such as walking can actually reduce inflammation in some joints and thereby reduce the pain rather than make it worse. A programme that includes stretching, aerobic exercises and basic strength training (see Chapter 14) is best.

Why do I have to build muscles? It's my joints that hurt.

When you have OA, you don't have to exercise to get in shape, you have to get in shape to exercise. Before a person with OA in their knees or hips can comfortably exercise, they have to strengthen their muscles, and build up their range of motion.

How can stretching help?

When a joint hurts, you don't feel like moving it. But when you don't move it, the joint gets increasingly stiff, making any form of exercise unbearable.

That's where gentle stretches can help: they improve your flexibility and increase your range of motion. And better flexibility and range of motion mean that you can perform tasks that many people take for granted, but that those with OA may find difficult, such as reaching overhead for something off a top shelf, or turning your neck to see what's behind you.

Begin your stretches in the morning, when you are warm. A bath or a shower is a good place to start. Begin with the neck and jaw, and work your way to your feet, systematically stretching each muscle group as you go. Move slowly, and hold each position comfortably for 10-20 seconds. This should take less than 5 minutes.

Yoga provides a good opportunity to improve your flexibility. It's also an excellent form of relaxation. Just make sure that your instructor understands your special needs, and talk to your GP before starting any exercise programme.

Strengthening the muscles around an arthritic joint supports the joint and lessens the pain. For example, strengthening the quadriceps muscles, a group of muscles that cover the front of each thigh, helps stabilize the knee joint.

With help from your GP, you can choose from an array of strengthening options, including elastic bands, resistive water exercises (see Chapter 13), exercise machines and free weights.

Do your strengthening programme two or three times a week, for 15-20 minutes per session. Anti-inflammatory medications taken several hours before exercising will help ease any stiffness you may be feeling.

Start strengthening exercises slowly with light weights. You want to feel muscle fatigue but not pain. Muscle fatigue goes away after you finish the exercise; pain may persist. Exercise should never be painful.

What kind of aerobic exercises are best?

Choose an exercise that you enjoy and that doesn't hurt. When you have arthritis, there's no gain in pain, and if you hurt you can't keep exercising. Swimming and aqua-aerobics or walking in water are excellent choices, as they allow you to burn calories without placing weight on sore joints.

If you like to walk, make sure you're wearing proper walking shoes or trainers with good heel and arch support. If your knees are unstable, you should stick to a smooth surface or a treadmill rather than difficult trails.

If you're new to aerobic exercise, start with only a few minutes a day, gradually increasing to 20-30 minutes daily. For great convenience, break it up into 5-minute intervals throughout the day. If you anticipate some stiffness or arthritic pain, take an over-the-counter pain reliever 15-30 minutes before starting.

CHAPTER 2

New Hope for Rheumatoid Arthritis?

A host of new therapies can ease the pain and disability of this damaging disease

Diane Gru woke up one morning with red painful wrists. As pain and inflammation jumped from her wrists to her fingers and toes, Gru, who works as a teacher, visited a GP who recommended that she visit an Early Arthritis Clinic at her local hospital. Both her and her doctor's quick actions proved to be vital. She was found to be suffering from rheumatoid arthritis (RA).

Diet forms an important part of controlling RA

Tune Out Rheumatoid Arthritis Pain

For those with rheumatoid arthritis, even simple daily activities can be painful. Exercise can seem impossible, yet it is often exactly what doctors recommend to improve mobility. The key to staying active may be music.

In a small study at Glasgow University, researchers found that women with RA could walk 30% further when they listened to music of their choice than when they walked in silence. "The music didn't make their pain disappear," says lead researcher Dr Paul MacIntyre. "It took their mind off it, so they could walk further without needing to stop."

RA is an auto-immune disease, characterized by inflammation of the lining of the joints. It affects more than a million people in the UK, most of them women between the ages of 20 and 45. For reasons that are not fully understood, the body's immune system turns against itself and attacks healthy joint tissue.

The resulting inflammation can lead to irreversible destruction of bone and cartilage. And it can be disabling: around half the people diagnosed with RA are unable to work within 10 years of the onset of the disease.

But because she was diagnosed early, this wasn't the case for Gru. She started on a programme of drug therapy immediately, and after trying different medications, she found the ones that took away her pain and slowed the disease. "I can do anything I used to do," says Gru. That includes exercising, a combination of yoga, step aerobics, treadmill, and stairclimber at her gym, as well as playing the piano.

What causes RA?

Genes play a big role in determining who does and doesn't get RA, but they don't provide all the answers. One theory is that environmental factors, such as a virus or a bacteria, 'turn on' RA in people with an inherited susceptibility.

How is it treated?

It used to be standard for doctors to put off prescribing more powerful drugs for as long as

TAKE CONTROL

Cutting out problem foods

If you think that you have a food sensitivity, start a food diary to keep track of what you were eating around the time a flare-up occurred. If you discover a pattern—you were eating eggs just before an attack—you'll have an idea of what to avoid in the future. Once you have a possible culprit, stop eating that food for five days. Then try the food again and see if the symptoms reappear.

Boost Your Immunity

As rheumatoid arthritis is an auto-immune disease, it makes sense to take steps to get your immune system working as efficiently, and, more importantly, as correctly as possible. Here are a few tips to help your immune system do what it is supposed to be doing.

Veg out: Eat as many fruits and vegetables as you can. Nutrition experts recommend that we eat five portions of health-giving fruits and vegetables a day. Most of us are lucky if we get three—and that's why so many people are overweight, tired, and ill. Make it your daily goal to meet, and if possible beat, the minimum requirement.

Every piece of veg counts

Supplement it: It's difficult to ensure that you're getting all the nutrients you need from your diet. A multi-vitamin is your insurance policy—so look for one that tops up your calcium and vitamins E, C, and D. Vitamin D in particular is the key to building strong bones and may play a role in keeping arthritis in check. Experts recommend 10 mcg of vitamin D a day, the amount found in many multivitamins.

Move about: Just 30 minutes of exercise a day will boost your immune system, improve your stamina, make you stronger, cheer you up, and stretch stiff joints and muscles. A walk is all you need.

Sleep on it: Most of us get an average of 6 hours and 40 minutes of sleep during the working week. But for a full restorative night's shut-eye, you need eight hours. So treat yourself.

Water yourself: Water is one of nature's most important nutrients—and one that most people don't get enough of. Aim for 8 to 10 240 ml glasses of water a day to keep you well hydrated. Count tea, coffee, or cola as half, as the caffeine acts as a diuretic. And drink an extra glass of water for every boozy drink you have during the day.

Join Club Med

Look hard enough and you'll find plenty of alternative remedies suggested for the treatment of RA. Unfortunately, few have been scientifically tested. One that has, though, is the Mediterranean diet.

Scientists have long been interested in the apparent healthiness and longevity of people in the Med, so they've studied the effects of their typical diet: One that's rich in fruits and vegetable, olive oil, and fresh fish. And the results have been extremely promising for RA sufferers.

One Greek study, published in the 'American Journal of Clinical Nutrition', found that people with the lowest lifetime consumption of extra virgin olive oil had a two-and-half times greater chance of developing RA than those with the highest.

And another study found that eating the Mediterranean way seemed to relieve pain, stiffness, and hand weakness from RA by up to 38%. Bonus: The same diet has also been found to cut heart attack risk, which is doubled in those with RA.

Start cooking with olive oil

possible to spare patients some of the worst side effects, which can include liver and kidney damage, as well as blood problems.

Now that they know that RA can cause permanent disability within a few years, or even months, doctors are quickly putting patients on what are called disease-modifying, anti-rheumatic drugs (DMARD), a more aggressive therapy that's now the gold standard in RA patient care.

If you have RA, the chances are that you will be taking at least two different kinds of medication: those that reduce your symptoms, such as non-steroidal anti-inflammatories (NSAIDs) or corticosteroids, and those that slow progression of the disease before the joints are damaged (the DMARDS).

While NSAIDs and steroids provide fast relief, DMARDS work over time, sometimes taking several weeks to several months before patients and their doctors know if they're going to help. They're often used in combination with other RA medication.

Most DMARDs, in use for decades, were used to treat other diseases, and their effect against RA was only discovered accidentally. Among the most commonly prescribed are methotrexate, a cancer drug, and sulfasaline, also used to treat bowel disease. Leflunomide is one of the newest DMARDs, and was specifically developed for treating RA. It inhibits the immune system, which is involved in the inflammatory process. Several other drugs used to treat RA, including methotrexate, also target the immune system.

DMARDS have been life-savers for many people with RA, bringing relief from symptoms and slowing down the disease. But they often have intolerable side effects, and none has produced what rheumatologists and their patients have been searching for: long-term remission.

What about the newer DMARDs?

The newest DMARDs may solve some of these problems. They're so different that they have their own classification, TNF blockers. Since 1998, the first three Tumor Necrosos Factor (TNF) blockers have been introduced in the UK: etanercerpt, infliximab, and, most recently, adalimumab.

These so-called "biologics" interrupt the inflammation process by blocking the action of certain proteins associated with swelling and joint damage in people with RA. Called cytokines, these proteins seem to be more abundant in people with RA than others. Unlike most other RA medication, the biologics aren't pills. They're proteins that must be taken either by self-injection, in the same way that diabetics take insulin, or by intravenous infusion, which must be done by a doctor. But the biggest difference between biologics and DMARDs is that biologics have fewer side effects. That's because they target specific components of the immune system that contribute to RA, while leaving the other aspects of the immune system alone.

Have these new TNF blockers been proven to work?

Etanercerpt and infliximab—either alone or in combination with methodrexate, the tradtional drug, appear to work faster and may produce better results than methotrexate alone.

In a study done at the Johns Hopkins University in Baltimore, USA, for example, etanercerpt stopped the disease progression in

TNF blockers: The Newest RA Fighters

ETANERCEPT (ENBREL)

What it does: Delays structural damage and reduces signs and symptoms of moderately to severely active RA.

Who's getting it: People who haven't responded to other drugs; children with unresponsive juvenile RA; it can also be used to treat children with severe juvenile idiopathic arthritis, psoriatic arthritis, or ankylosing spondylitis.

Side effects: Local irritiation at site of injection; concerns that it curbs the inflammatory response, so it may make it harder to fight infection.

INFLIXIMAB (REMICADE)

What it does: Delays structural damage and reduces signs and symptoms of moderately to severely actice RA.

Who's getting it: Used in conjuction with methotrexate in people with moderate to severely active RA who haven't shown much improvement with methotrexate; people with ankylosing spondylitis; people with Crohn's disease.

Side effects: Same concerns about infection as with etanercept.

ADALIMUMAB (HUMIRA)

What it does: Reduces signs and symptoms of moderate to severe RA.

Who's getting it: Used alone or in combination with a DMARD such as methotrexate in people with moderate to severe RA.

Side effects: Minor reactions at injection site; concerns about infection.

Know the Symptoms

Diagnosing rheumatoid arthritis (RA) can be challenging. Many of RA's hallmark signs and symptoms, such as fatigue and joint pain, are shared by other health conditions, including other forms of arthritis. Also, symptoms may come and go early on, making diagnosis difficult.

RA typically involves the same joints on both sides of the body. The hands, wrists, feet, knees, ankles, shoulders, neck, jaw, and elbows may be affected.

Here are a few of the symptoms that rheumatologists will look for when evaluating patients for RA:

➤ Morning stiffness in and around joints lasting at least one hour before maximum improvement.

➤ At least three joint areas with simultaneous soft tissue swelling or fluid.

➤ At least one joint area swollen in a wrist, knuckle, or the middle joint of a finger.

➤ Simultaneous involvement of the same joint areas on both sides of the body.

➤ Rheumatoid nodules (lumps of tissue) under the skin.

➤ Rheumatoid factor in the blood. (Approximately 80% of people with RA test positive for the presence of rheumatoid factor, an antibody found in the blood. However, the absence or presence of rheumatoid factor does not indicate that one has RA.)

➤ X-ray evidence of erosions (wearing away of the surface of the bone) is typical of rheumatoid arthritis in the hand or the joints

Other possible symptoms include loss of appetite, fever, loss of energy, and anaemia.

72% of the RA patients who injected it twice a week for a year, while just 60% had a similar improvement taking methotrexate pills.

One downside to biologics is that questions remain about their safety and long-term efficacy because they are so new. The most common side effects are susceptibility to infection, such as sinus infections, headaches, nausea, and redness, irritation or pain at the injection sites.

What treatment is right for me?

Of course, with more options, the decision on which treatment is best for you is more challenging. A lot will depend on the severity of your disease and how fast it progresses, how you respond to different treatments, and what side effects you feel.

Though the new medications are an exciting development, about two-thirds of people suffering from RA are already helped dramatically by traditional medications such as DMARDs and NSAIDs. If you're in the remaining third who aren't being helped by existing treatments, these new medications offer hope that you can stop RA from taking over your life.

Asserting Immunity

Since there is considerable evidence that RA is triggered by a faulty immune system, and as the immune system is affected by what we eat, it stands to reason that for some sufferers, diet can make a difference in how they feel. This is certainly the starting point for those looking for an alternative approach to treating RA.

"Diet can be critical in the treatment of rheumatoid arthritis," says Dr Joel Fuhrman, a

Leaky gut syndrome

Leaky gut syndrome, or intestinal hyperpermeability, is a condition that isn't widely recognized or tested for, but is an ailment that some doctors feel offers an explanation for the auto-immune activity seen in rheumatoid arthritis.

These doctors believe that proteins from animal-based foods can leak in their whole undigested form, from the intestine into the bloodstream. This prompts the body to react as if a foreign invader has entered the blood, and it starts producing antibodies.

This wouldn't normally be a problem, but for the fact that beef or milk protein is extremely similar to human protein. And as the antibodies can't tell the difference, they'll target the proteins in your joints too.

WHAT CAN YOU DO?

Eating an animal protein-free diet may help relieve the symptoms of RA. To test this approach, you'll have to avoid all animal foods, including meat, fish, eggs, and dairy products. Eat wholegrains, seeds, pulses, nuts, and vegetables such as broccoli, sweetcorn, potatoes and peas for protein. Use soya milk fortified with calcium or vegetables such as kale, cauliflower and brussels sprouts for calcium.

Make broccoli your favourite veg

specialist in nutritional medicine. "In populations that consume natural diets of mostly unprocessed fruits, vegetables, and grains, auto-immune diseases are almost non-existent. You don't see much crippling rheumatoid arthritis in rural China, for example, because the people there eat differently that we do in the West."

More is involved than getting more fruits, vegetables and grains. (See Chapter 8 for more on the Ultimate Arthritis Diet). Some people are sensitive to certain foods—such as wheat, dairy foods, citrus fruits, tomatoes, or eggs—that can switch on the body's inflammatory response cutting them out can help to relieve the symptoms.

CHAPTER 3

Fight Back Against Fibromyalgia

Learn how to turn off the pain, fatigue, and frustration of this condition

You're not crazy. We all need to hear those words from time to time. But for people with the often frustrating, sometimes frightening, condition called fibromyalgia syndrome (FMS), it can take many years and several doctors to get a clean bill of mental health.

Fibromyalgia is a ghost of an ailment; it can cause life-disturbing pain, but it remains invisible to conventional diagnostic tests. Without hard data to study, the medical community has also been slow to admit that fibromyalgia is real, but it also offers hope in beating the pain. And people seeking relief from FMS have more options than ever before.

Learn to take things gently and relax

What is Fibromyaglia?

There are no clear statistics on the number of fibromyalgia syndrome (FMS) suffers in the UK, but it's clear that hundreds of thousands are afflicted by the condition. Most are women between the ages of 20 and 50, although it can also affect men, the elderly, and children. FMS is a type of rheumatism, and although the pain profile varies from person to person, typical symptoms take the form of intense burning or aching sensations in various muscles throughout the body, often accompanied by stiffness. Another hallmark of FMS is extreme fatigue; the pain prevents restful sleep. The pain itself can be intense, may be felt everyday, and can continue unabated for months.

Unlike other forms of arthritis, fibromyalgia doesn't produce pain or swelling in the joints. In fact, people suffering from the condition are often said to look well physically, even though they feel terrible. As a consequence, the usual tools for detecting the disease also fail to show anything is wrong. That's why, in the past, some doctors were certain that the condition was a psychological problem rather than a physical one. It turns out the patients were right all along.

Do you have fibromyalgia?

Doctors will most likely diagnose fibromyalgia if you have had widespread muscle pain for three months or more, and specific pain in 11 of 18 tender points (see below). If pressing on the tender points causes pain, you may have fibromyalgia.

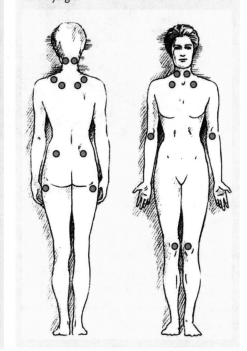

What causes FMS?

Ask the experts what causes fibromyalgia—what's happening in the body to produce pain, fatigue, and other symptoms—and you get a resigned, if considered, shrug.

There are a couple of different theories. For example, a study presented in 2000 suggests that in people with FMS, the central nervous system—the brain and spinal cord—doesn't process pain signals normally. In the study, researchers applied heat to the hands of a group of FMS patients and a group of healthy subjects. In the FMS patients, the blips of pain from each jolt of heat didn't subside between applications the way they did in the healthy group. Instead, the nervous system held onto the pain signals, and the

Relax and put your feet up to eliminate stress

sensations accumulated, causing the FMS patients to report feeling more pain than the control group.

We are constantly exposed to stimuli as we go through our day, and this inability to let go may contribute to the constant state of pain in people with FMS. But what causes a person's nervous system to behave like this is still very much a mystery.

Another body of research into FMS has looked closely at sleep patterns. Brain wave studies of people suffering from FMS show that they lose deep sleep, which is often disturbed by lighter, dreaming sleep. To support this theory, some researchers have demonstrated that otherwise healthy people who are woken in the middle of deep sleep demonstrate many of the symptoms of FMS.

TAKE CONTROL

Relieve pain naturally

Try meditation to take away the pain. A recent study at the University of Missouri found that a combination of exercise and the cognitive-behavioral therapy techniques of meditation and relaxation provides more symptom relief than anti-depressants, NSAIDS, or muscle relaxants.

Exercise carefully

Exercise plays a key role in managing FMS. Some of the most encouraging studies show that regular exercise can produce impressive improvements in the pain of FMS sufferers. What's more, an exercise regime not only has physical benefits, but also boosts morale.

In a recent study, women on an easy walking programme for 24 weeks reduced their symptoms by 54 per cent. "The key is to exercise smartly," says the project's lead researcher, Barbara Meyer from the University of Wisconsin in the USA. Here's her advice about how to approach exercise safely and effectively.

Warm up with water

A bath or shower relaxes muscles, increases circulation, and can make exercise feel easier.

Break it up

Forget traditional exercise guidelines. You need longer recovery and you may have trouble sustaining activity. Try gentle walking for 5 minutes three times a day, and build from there. (See Chapter 12 for a beginner's walking plan.)

Do brief stretches

Stretching promotes circulation and maintains your range of motion. But stick with short stretches, holding 5-10 seconds, so you don't stress your muscles.

Keep strong with tubing

Eccentric contractions, those your muscles perform while lowering weights such as dumbbells, can exacerbate FMS. Instead, use resistance tubes or bands, which are gentle and offer softer resistance. (For supplies of resistance tubing, visit **www.dietandfitnessresources.co.uk**.)

Aim low

FMS causes many tender points in the torso. For sustained aerobic exercise, focus on lower body activities such as cycling or walking.

Stop before fatigue sets in

You can exercise through normal pain, but stop when you feel you can go just a little longer. That way, you'll be able to exercise tomorrow as well.

Listen to your body

It's okay to exercise or be active while you're feeling the pain level that you typically experience from FMS. But if exercising causes your pain levels to become more intense, back off, and try a lighter workload when you're ready.

Keep stretching light and gentle

Don't be afraid

Exercise is difficult for some FMS patients not only because of the pain, but because their body can feel fragile. But while pain is usually a warning sign, the muscle pain of FMS is a symptom of illness. There's no evidence that people with FMS are more susceptible to injury than non-sufferers.

Fast facts

Recognize the symptoms of FMS
- ➤ General aching, stiffness, or tenderness in at least three specific sites around the body
- ➤ Pain that persists for at least three months
- ➤ Constant interruption of sleep
- ➤ Lack of energy and a general feeling of fatigue
- ➤ Stiff and painful muscles when immobile for any time period

What causes the disturbance of deep sleep is another point of conjecture; pain or stiffness in the neck, stress of another injury, disease, or depression and anxiety are all potential triggers.

Once FMS sets in, there is a vicious cycle where increased pain causes greater sleep disturbance, which in turn leads to more pain.

How can I treat the condition and take control?

If you have a mysterious ailment that is difficult to diagnose, has an unknown cause, and isn't well understood, is there cause for hope? There's plenty. Less than 20% of people diagnosed with fibromyalgia are disabled by it, and many get better over time. You can tilt the odds in your favour by following these simple suggestions:

Find a savvy doctor

One of the most important things to do is find a sympathetic doctor, who can give you the information you need, and support you in self-care. Because not all remedies work for everyone, you have to communicate with your doctor to find a regime that helps you.

Take the medication

Your doctor may recommend a programme of painkillers and NSAIDS, and will likely try to help with your sleep disturbance.

Seek out support

Many people with FMS have never met anyone else with the condition. If you communicate with other sufferers, you won't feel so alone. Just remember to focus on solutions, not problems.

Monitor your diet

Eat healthily to keep your weight down (see Chapter 8), and avoid drinks such as alcohol, tea, and coffee late at night.

Identify the stress

Try to find the points of stress in your life—be it work, family, or relationship—and address the problem.

Take the long view

Don't be over-ambitious about your progress and don't expect immediate results. It takes time to build up an exercise programme and time for the symptoms of the condition to abate. FMS can be severe and may last for years, but many people have learnt to control the condition successfully.

Nutrition advice for FMS

"If you have fibromyalgia, you're at great risk for poor nutrition," says Dr Rachel Trevethan, a nutritionist. When symptoms flare up, eating right becomes less of a priority. Trevethan, who specializes in giving nutrition advice to people with fibromyalgia, makes the following suggestions.

Eat to sleep

Sleep is a precious commodity for FMS sufferers. Avoid sleep-busters such as caffeine and alcohol for at least 5 hours before going to bed. For a sleep-promoting bedtime snack, try a bowl of wholegrain cereal sprinkled with fruit, or a bowl of warm oatmeal.

Keep a record

Many people with FMS experience irritable bowel symptoms such as diarrhoea or upset stomach. Keeping a record of what foods you eat can help you identify and avoid the foods that trigger these symptoms.

Plan ahead

People with fibromyalgia typically have good days and bad days. "When you're feeling better, prepare some meals in advance, and keep them in the fridge or freezer," says Trevethan. You may not feel like chopping vegetables when your pain flares up, but if there's a salad already made, you'll be less tempted to order a pizza (or you'll order a smaller one).

Graze, don't gorge

Eating several snacks and small meals every day instead of a few large spreads gives your body a constant energy supply. For at least three of these mealettes, include milk, carbohydrates (wholegrains, fruits, or vegetables), and mono unsaturated fats (nuts, olives, or avocados). "Eat when you're hungry; stop before you're overfull," says Trevethan. For most people, that means munching every 3 hours or so.

Keep a journal of your eating habits

Be sensibly skeptical

"There's a lot of misinformation about fibromyalgia," says Trevethan, which is not surprising, since there are so many unanswered questions about it. Be sceptical about anything pitched at you as a miracle cure – it won't be.

CHAPTER 4

Demystifying AS

Recognize the warning signs of Ankylosing Spondylitis, then use this mobility programme to beat its debilitating effects

nkylosing Spondylitis (AS) is a painful, progressive inflammatory rheumatic disease that affects one in 200 men and one in 500 women in the UK, most often in their late teens and early 20s. Only rarely does it begin after the age of 45. The condition mainly affects the spine, but it can also affect other joints, tendons and ligaments, and possibly eyes, lungs, heart, and bowel. AS causes bones to fuse together. Ligaments or tendons become inflamed where they attach to bone, and as this subsides and the healing process begins, new bone develops.

Young and at risk from AS...

As the flexible tissue of ligaments and tendons are replaced with bone, it becomes more difficult to move. In men, it most often starts at the pelvis, then moves up through the lower back, chest wall, and neck. For women, it is more likely to affect the knees, ankles, hips, and feet.

What causes AS?

No one is exactly sure. Research indicates that genetics are a major factor. Most people with AS have a gene called HLA-B27. This is twice as common in people of northern European descent as in those of Afro-Caribbean heritage, although not everyone with the gene has the condition.

Sometimes a bowel infection can trigger AS, as can a group of symptoms known as Reiter's Syndrome. These include iritis and uveitis (see 'How does AS affect other organs?'), conjunctivitis and urethritis (inflammation of the urethra—the tube that carries urine from the bladder out of the body). Reiter's Syndrome can also spark arthritis.

What are the symptoms of AS?

The first sign of a problem could be a dull ache all across the buttock area. It might intermittently move from one side to the other. These early pains are often indicative of sacroiliitis, the inflammation of the sacroiliac joints.

Over time, as the inflammation extends to the spine, the lower back will become stiff and painful. Sufferers are likely to feel stiff in the morning, but improve throughout the day with exercise and stretching.

The condition can deteriorate as the back pains become chronic, although it's also common to have periods of relatively pain-free remission. Weight loss, fatigue, night sweats, and broken sleep often accompany the early symptoms. Although the course of AS varies with each individual, most people with the disease continue to live a normal and productive life, although they generally have to modify their lifestyle or their work.

How can AS affect other organs?

Eyes

AS can cause the iris to become inflamed, in particular the uvea, which attaches it to the outer wall of the eye. If you develop iritis or uveitis, initially your vision may become blurred, then there will be a sharp pain and your eye will become badly bloodshot. If this happens, go straight to casualty and tell the doctors that you have AS; they will give you eye drops that will reduce the inflammation and avoid any permanent damage.

Heart

Very occasionally, AS can affect the electrical activity of the heart, or cause the aortic valve to leak, but this is very rare, and usually so mild that the patient may not even notice the symptoms.

Lungs

If your rib joints are affected by AS, breathing, sneezing, and coughing can be painful, and your lungs may not get fully ventilated. There are exercises you can do to maintain normal chest wall movement (see panel, page 32), but in later stages of the disease, the chest wall can become extremely stiff, so that only the diaphragm can move. This means that eating large meals or wearing tight clothing can make breathing uncomfortable. If you smoke, giving up will help.

Try these two simple exercises to help extend your spine and help your chest expansion.

Lie face down on your front (preferably on a bed, although the floor will also suffice), stretch your arms out at shoulder level, and raise chest, shoulders, arms, and head off the ground as far as possible. Hold for 5 seconds, relax and repeat 20 times.

To perform a standing corner press-up, bend your elbows and lean forward towards the corner of a wall with your head, neck, and spine fully extended. Keep your knees firmly planted on the floor. Hold for a count for a count of 5, push up and straighten your arms, relax, and repeat 20 times.

How is AS diagnosed?

The non-specific nature of the initial back pain can make the early diagnosis difficult, particularly if it is interspersed with periods of remission.

In a full and thorough examination, your GP should look for pain or tenderness in the sacroiliac joints (to help confirm sacroiliitis) and measure spinal mobility. Your GP should also check your posture to see if the lumbar spine is beginning to flatten out, and may refer you to a rheumatologist for X-rays and a further examination.

How is AS treated?

There is currently no preventative measure or cure for Ankylosing Spondylitis. Normally, patients take non-steroidal anti-inflammatory drugs (NSAIDs) to reduce inflammation and ease pain and stiffness.

Ankylosing Spondylitis is also increasingly treated with disease-modifying anti-rheumatic drugs (DMARDs), and the good news is that there have been some promising early results for those treated with anti-TNF therapy (see chapter 5 for more about this.)

Fighting back against AS

The course of the disease varies according to the individual; the early symptoms may come and go, but for most people, they become persistent. In the later stages, the pain may also have spread from the lower back to the upper part of the back and shoulders. Regular exercise is widely recommended in the long-term management of the disease as a complement to, rather than replacement for, pain-relieving medication.

The following muscle-strengthening and stretching programme was developed to improve the mobility of the back, hips, shoulders, and other joints associated with the ongoing development of AS. They will help to keep the spine mobile and erect, and to maintain a good range of joint movement. Since most AS-sufferers find it difficult to exercise first thing in the morning, it's a good idea to try the programme after a warm bath or shower. As with all exercise programmes, start slowly and build up gradually. Try to do the exercises at least once a day; ideally twice. Repeat each exercise at least 5 times, and try to also do some other form of exercise at least once a day that has you out of breath for at least 5 minutes.

1 Taking care not to strain your back, lift your hips off the floor as high as possible, hold for 5 seconds and slowly lower.

2 Keep your elbows straight throughout, tuck your head and arch your back high (making an "n" shape). Then lift your head and lower your back deeply (making a "u" shape).

3 Keep your head up, raise your right arm forwards and your left leg backwards as far as possible. Keep your shoulders and hips square to the ground. Hold for 5 seconds, return to all fours and lift your left arm and right leg.

4 Sit on a stable chair with your feet hooked inside the legs. Hold the chair, then bend sideways as far as possible. Hold for 5 seconds and switch arms.

5 With your arms clasped on your forearms at shoulder level, turn your upper body to the right as far as possible. Hold, then repeat on the opposite side.

6 Holding the chair, turn your head to the right as far as possible without letting your shoulders turn. Repeat on the opposite side.

7 Place your heel on the seat of a chair, keep your knee straight and reach forward as far as you can with both hands. Try to keep your back straight. Hold for 6 seconds, relax and repeat with the opposite leg.

8 Face the side of a chair and hold the chair-back with your right hand. Bend your right knee and place your right shin on the seat. Repeat the move at least 5 times per leg.

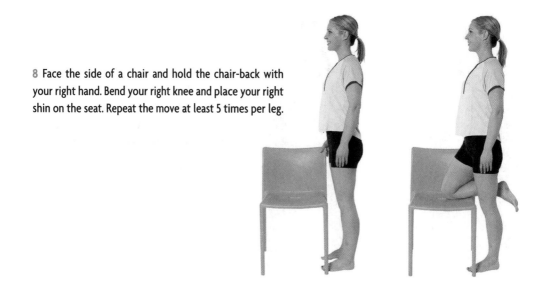

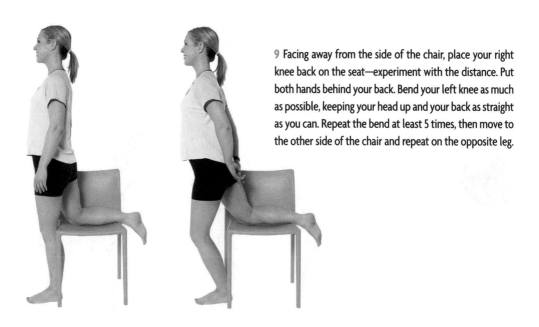

9 Facing away from the side of the chair, place your right knee back on the seat—experiment with the distance. Put both hands behind your back. Bend your left knee as much as possible, keeping your head up and your back as straight as you can. Repeat the bend at least 5 times, then move to the other side of the chair and repeat on the opposite leg.

10 Stand straight with your shoulders back and buttocks flat against a wall or in a line. Stretch up as tall as possible without lifting your heels. Lift your left arm while holding the other straight against your side. Hold, then repeat with the opposite arm. You can try the same exercise lying flat on the floor keeping your feet at right angles and the backs of your heels down.

Part 2

take control of your life

There is no cure for arthritis but you have a host of treatment options to help you live a happy and full life

CHAPTER 5

Medicines That Fight Arthritis

With the right medication, you can look forward to a pain-free and active life

There are more than 200 varieties of arthritis, and a bewildering range of drugs to treat them. Most are well-established and proven to be effective, while others are cutting-edge treatments that have only recently become available. Different people will respond differently to each type of medication, even if they have the same symptoms. For this reason, it's essential that when you are prescribed any sort of drug you keep a record of what you take, how it helps you, and any side-effects

Be sure to keep a medication diary

it has. Usually, arthritis sufferers take a combination of drugs to combat the disease itself, called first-line drugs, and others—second-line drugs—to control their symptoms. The types listed below are the most commonly prescribed.

Pain-killers

This category—sometimes referred to as "analgesics"—encompasses everything from the paracetamol you can buy in the chemist or supermarket through to the stronger medication, such as codeine, that only comes with a prescription. It also includes pain-relieving gels that you apply to the skin.

Non-steroidal anti-inflammatory drugs (NSAIDs)

NSAIDs are the most commonly prescribed medication to treat the symptoms of arthritis. They are used to reduce stiffness and swelling in arthritic joints—in fact, they're vital in relieving the most debilitating symptoms of all forms of the condition. Non-steroidal anti-inflammatory drugs include ibuprofen and aspirin. They are second-line drugs, and so have no impact on the long-term effects of the disease.

As the name suggests, NSAIDs do not contain steroids, and so do not carry some of the risks—such as osteoporosis—associated with other medications. However, they do have their own possible side-effects, in particular on the stomach. Some people experience tummy upsets or indigestion with NSAIDs, and with large doses or prolonged use, they can damage the lining of your stomach. You may not be able to use NSAIDs if you have a history of stomach ulcers or asthma.

A new category of NSAIDs—COX-2s inhibitors—have recently become available. COX-2s inhibitors do not cause the digestive problems that commonly occur with other NSAIDs, so if you are finding your medication hard to stomach, ask your doctor about them.

NSAIDs provide vital relief

Disease modifying anti-rheumatic drugs (DMARDs)

DMARDs are used to treat the types of arthritis that are diseases of the immune system, such as rheumatoid arthritis. Because they are first-line drugs, they can retard the progress of the disease. So, once you have been diagnosed, doctors will often prescribe relatively strong doses of DMARDs to try to prevent irreversible damage to your joints. It can take weeks, or even months, for the drugs to have their full effect, and because there can be serious side-effects, anyone taking DMARDs must be monitored by their doctor.

Immunosuppressive drugs are one of the main types of DMARDs. As the name suggests, they suppress the immune system, lowering your blood count and making you more susceptible to infection. If you are taking one of these sorts of DMARDs and you get a sore throat

Ease drug side effects

Most powerful drugs cause side effects, and the more you take and the higher the dose, the higher your risk. But you can help cut down on your risk—and continue to reap all the drugs' benefits—with these simple strategies:

Exercise

Aerobic exercise and strength training build your muscles so that they can better support and protect your joints, thereby easing your pain. Aerobic exercise and simple stretching (see page 98) can also ease stiffness and accompanying pain. It will also help you keep your weight stable.

Stay Trim

Extra pounds put extra stress on your joints, causing pain and increasing your risk of further damage to the cartilage inside. Take care of your diet, as well as your exercise routine.

Learn To Relax

Stress hurts in a number of ways. When you are under strain, you perceive pain more intensely than you do when you're relaxed. Stress can make you tense your muscles, worsening the pain. It can also undercut your ability to cope with pain and just about everything else. To relax and get relief, try these tips:

> ➤ Learn a relaxation technique, such as deep breathing, for when stress and pain levels rise.
> ➤ Try to identify the things that are making you feel stressed; then try to change the ones you can change.
> ➤ Talk to your family, friends, and colleagues about how they can help.

or mouth ulcers, or develop unexplained bruising or bleeding, you should talk to your doctor as soon as you can. If you come into contact with someone who has chickenpox, you should see your doctor immediately, as you may need special treatment should you catch it from them.

Certain immunosuppressants can have side effects. For example, cyclophosphamide can cause cystitis—inflammation and bleeding of the bladder—and cyclosporin can affect your blood pressure and your kidneys. If you develop any medical problems when you start taking your medication, go straight back to your doctor.

Steroids

Steroids are man-made versions of hormones that occur naturally in the body. They are used to reduce inflammation, which they do to great effect, but like NSAIDs, they cannot cure

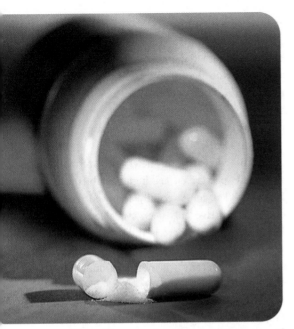

arthritis. They can be taken as tablets, or if the swelling is very localized, injected into the affected joint or to the soft tissue surrounding it.

Some of the side effects of steroids can be severe, resulting in, for example, osteoporosis (weakening of the bones). Often, your doctor will recommend that you take a course of calcium tablets to minimize the chances of osteoporosis. Other problems could be weight gain, stomach pains, mood swings, and a puffy face. The likelihood and the severity of these effects increases with dose and the length of time you take steroids, so your doctor will always prescribe you the lowest-strength tablets or injection that will work for you. If you have to take steroids for a prolonged period, it is likely that your dose will have to be increased over time. As with all drugs, you and your doctor must talk through the pros and cons of each medication to decide what is right for you.

When you start taking steroids, you will feel the benefits within days. Because

steroids have such a profound effect on the body, it is important that in the event of an accident, any doctor who treats you can quickly understand your situation. You should carry a Steroid Card, which details your medication dosage.

Remember:

Always follow the specific instructions that come with each type of medication: what time of day it should be taken; whether it should be taken with food or on an empty stomach; if you should avoid alcohol.

If you experience side effects from your medication, consult your doctor immediately.

If you want to use over-the-counter medicines, talk to the pharmacist or your doctor and explain what you take on prescription so they can advise you. Likewise, talk to your doctor about holiday vaccinations.

Take the right dose at the right frequency —if you miss any, don't try to "catch up"; resume your usual pattern as soon as you can.

Don't share your medication with anyone, even if they seem to have exactly the same symptoms as you do.

If you are pregnant, planning to become pregnant, or breast-feeding, ask your doctor how your medication could affect you and your baby.

Don't stop taking your medication part-way through a course without consulting your doctor.

If you have any uncertainties about what you're taking, talk to your doctor and don't be afraid to ask all the questions you want to.

Your doctor is there to help

Anti-TNFs

TNF stands for Tumor Necrosos Factor, a kind of protein from the cytokine family that is associated with the inflammation of rheumatoid arthritis. Doctors don't know why, but RA sufferers seem to have more of these proteins than normal. By blocking them with anti-TNF drugs, these effects can be countered.

Anti-TNFs are still new, and are not as widely prescribed as better-established DMARDs. The most recently approved types of anti-TNFs have only been available in the UK since 2003, so there is little information about the possible long-term effects they might have. Doctors will normally only prescribe anti-TNFs to patients who have not responded well to other types of medication. Anti-TNFs are not usually suitable for patients who have previously had, or currently have, cancer or tuberculosis, or other persistently recurring infections.

Unlike most other arthritis medication, anti-TNFs are injected. Some types can be self-administered, or a family member or partner can be trained to do it for you. For other types, such as infliximab, you will need to go to hospital as an outpatient to receive your drugs intravenously. Initially, you will have to go every couple of weeks for this, then once every 8 weeks.

Anti-TNFs are not designed to alleviate pain, though of course, as they reduce inflammation, your discomfort should lessen. Your doctor is likely to keep you on any painkillers that you are taking before you begin a course of anti-TNFs.

CHAPTER 6

How Surgery Can Get You Back on Your Feet Again

Far from being a worst-case scenario, surgery could be your route to a new life without pain

No matter how early it is diagnosed, nor how carefully you may use conventional and complementary therapies, surgery is sometimes the only way to overcome arthritis. But don't let your doctor saying "operation" send you into a panic—there are many surgical techniques that are proven to reduce pain and increase mobility in arthritis sufferers, and many are simple procedures.

Simple operations can put a spring in your step

How do you know if it's time for surgery?

Surgery may be a decision that is made for you with a recommendation from your GP and a consultation with an orthopaedic surgeon. However, it's something that should be on your mind if you notice a combination of the following:

➤ The pain prevents you from sleeping with any regularity at night.
➤ You feel that the pain from arthritis is preventing you from leaving your house to visit family or friends, or from doing simple household tasks such as shopping.
➤ Your prescribed medication is no longer providing pain relief.
➤ You struggle with daily life, you can't climb the stairs, get out of a chair or visit the toilet without great difficulty.

Joint replacement

Around 50,000 people in the UK have joint replacement surgery every year. Most of these operations are to replace knees and hips, but shoulder joints are also commonly done. On average, an artificial joint—normally made of plastic, metal, or ceramic—will have a lifespan of up to 15 years. After that, it will need to be replaced again. Because subsequent operations are not as long-lasting, doctors will only suggest surgery for younger patients when all other options have been exhausted.

After having a hip replacement, you should experience an absence of pain as soon as the soreness caused by the surgery itself

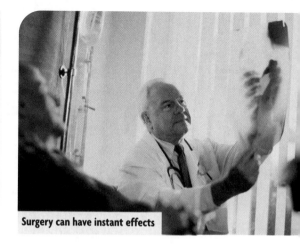

Surgery can have instant effects

has passed. But for hips, knees, shoulders, and elbows, remember that an artificial joint will never be as robust as the original. Knee surgery takes longer to recover from than hip operations, and is not a miracle cure. You will still have to consider weight loss (if you are overweight) to reduce stress on your new knees, and exercising to maintain muscle strength around the joint. Of course, if the pain of an arthritic knee has made exercise difficult, having the surgery will make it easier for you to lead a more active lifestyle once you have recovered from the operation.

If you have a shoulder joint replaced, the result will be a great reduction in pain, and, over time, a greater range of movement. However, patients who have had replacement shoulders joints fitted are unlikely to be able to lift their arm higher than shoulder-height after the operation.

It's not until your hands become painful that you realize just how much you use them. Arthritis in the wrists and hands can be extremely debilitating for this very reason, and surgery to ameliorate symptoms is carried out by specialists.

Hip resurfacing

A new technique to repair damaged joints—hip resurfacing—was approved by the National Institute for Clinical Excellence (NICE) in 2002. It is particularly useful for younger patients, as it makes any surgery that may be necessary in decades to come more straightforward. Preserving as much of the original bone as possible, surgeons resurface the hip joint and the hip socket with metal.

Synovectomy

Even if your bones are okay, if the lining of the joint around them—the synovium—is inflamed, movement will be painful and difficult, and it can accelerate the deterioration of the bone. Normally, this inflammation can be reduced by medication, but an alternative is synovectomy, in which the tissue is removed. If your drug treatment is not working, this can be done as keyhole surgery, and so is not too invasive.

TAKE CONTROL

Drop Some Pounds

Being overweight can put an extra strain on your heart and lungs during surgery. It can also slow down your recovery and put unnecessary strain on your new artificial joints. Try to lose some weight before surgery with a sensible dietary plan—don't diet in the month before your surgery—and take to the swimming pool for some simple non-weight-bearing exercise. (See chapter 13)

Arthrodesis/fusion

For some very painful and immobile joints, your doctor could suggest an operation to fuse bones together. This will of course mean that you can no longer move the joint, but for smaller bones—especially those in the toes, ankles, fingers, and

---

CASE STUDY
Ronnie Watts

Inevitably, the kind of work you do, or the lifestyle you lead, can make you more prone to wear-and-tear arthritis. Ronnie Watts has always loved to be her own boss, and she ran her own catering business for many years. Never one to sit behind a desk, she spent long hours on her feet every day, involved in all aspects of the business. Her feet became more and more painful, but she was so busy with her work that she didn't take time off to rest, or find out what was really wrong. When the pain got unbearable she went to the doctor, and was referred to a surgeon.

"It went on for years before I saw anyone," she says. "In the end, I couldn't even wear shoes, my feet were so distorted and painful." The surgeon operated immediately. "My joints were so calcified they had to be removed and replaced with metal clips. I was in plaster for three months," she says. The toe bones were realigned, so Ronnie's feet are back to their normal shape, with only discreet scarring underneath. She still has mild arthritis in many other joints, but takes flax oil and glucosamine—in combination with chondroitin sulphate, which has been proven to ease joint pain and stiffness, as well as protecting joint cartilage—regularly, and plays tennis and golf to keep in shape. She says the only problem she has now is that the metal in her toes sets off the detectors at airports.

wrists—it is a option worth considering, as it will strengthen the joint, enable it to bear weight better, and eliminate pain permanently. There are only two bones in your feet—your ankle and big toe joint—that can be replaced at all, so fusing is a good alternative for severely arthritic feet that need surgery. Sometimes an orthopaedic surgeon will suggest arthrodesis if you have badly damaged vertebrae in your neck, as it will lessen the likelihood of injuring the nerves.

Carpal tunnel syndrome

Carpal tunnel syndrome is common among people who work with computers, or with their hands. Tissues in the wrist swell, pressing on the median nerve, which runs up your forearm. This causes pain and numbness in the hand. By cutting the band of tissue at the affected place—again, this can be done by keyhole surgery—the symptoms can be relieved.

Other surgery

There are other minor procedures that can help your arthritis, some of which won't even mean an overnight stay in hospital. Even something straightforward, such as removing bunions, can make walking easier. Surgeons can "clean out" arthritic joints using keyhole surgery to remove torn cartilage and other debris. They can repair tendons, drain or remove cysts on the wrist joint, or use keyhole techniques to investigate and then assess damage to a joint.

CASE STUDY
Brenda Green

For some 69-year-olds, getting a little stiff in the hip might be accepted with a sigh as "part of the ageing process." But then, most 69-year-olds probably don't teach aerobics and yoga classes and compete in international athletics competitions. Brenda Green, who is now 74, has been a competitive runner for more than 20 years, and when her arthritis became so painful that she feared she may have to stop, she and her husband set out to find a cure.

"I didn't want a hip replacement—that might have put paid to my sprinting," she says. "But it was so painful, and worst during the night. I couldn't lie on one side, I couldn't get comfy." By chance, they heard about hip resurfacing, which had been carried out only a handful of times in the UK. Brenda went to the orthopaedic surgeon to see if she could have the operation.

Initially, she was told she was too old for the op, and that her bones would be too weak. But when she was X-rayed, the surgeon changed his mind. Years of running had kept them strong. "He told me I had the bones of a 32-year-old," she says.

Eight days after the operation, Brenda came home determined to do all the exercises she had been set, and made a rapid recovery. She started walking round the block, first with two crutches, then one, then unaided, and when she felt strong enough, went back to the running track. "The operation was in the October, and in the February I won the British 200m Championships," she says. Since the operation, Brenda has won the 70-74 age group European Indoor 400m title, and got a bronze medal in the 400m at last year's World Championships. Next year, she will go up an age group, and she is already looking forward to setting new records.

CHAPTER 7

An Alternative Approach to Pain Relief

The promise of pain relief free from side effects is turning more arthritis suffers on to complementary medicine

According to a recent study, one third of people in Great Britain say that they have tried complementary therapies, and of those suffering from arthritis, the figure is close to 60%.

People using complementary therapies believe there are times when Mother Nature knows best. Many chronic conditions appear to respond favourably to complementary treatment. Although there is no scientific evidence to support many of these therapies, a reduction in pain and discomfort, freedom from side effects and an enhanced quality of life are reported by many arthritis sufferers who've tried this approach to their treatment.

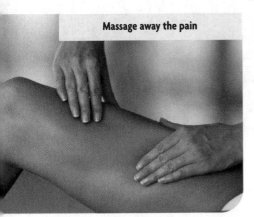

Massage away the pain

What is it?

The philosophy of complementary medicine is to encourage the body to gently heal itself. It looks at the whole person: the practitioner studies the background and lifestyle of the individual patient and considers those issues when diagnosing and prescribing. It is known as the holistic approach. Therefore, many therapies and remedies act on a multi-functional level—a treatment for the musclo-skeletal system may also benefit the heart, respiration, and skin.

Better all-round?

According to its proponents, the beauty of complementary therapy (experts call it CAM, short for complementary and alternative medicine) is that it encourages you to take responsibility for your own health; to promote wellness and prevent illness before it sets in. Bearing in mind the queues in doctors' waiting rooms, this would appear to be a sensible way forward. In fact, the Prince of Wales's Foundation for Integrated Health (he's a committed supporter) reports that a recent study by Sheffield University found that half of GP practices in England are making complementary therapies available to their patients. So don't be afraid to ask your doctor.

Nature's medicine chest

The therapies most acknowledged for their benefits for arthritis are: nutritional medicine, using optimal vitamin and mineral supplementation to augment the diet (see Chapter 9); herbalism, which harnesses the power of plants and their properties; the unique practice of homeopathy, and the more

hands-on disciplines of acupuncture, reflexology, chiropractic treatment, as well as the Alexander Technique and massage.

HERBALISM
Herbs and Arthritis

The use of herbs for healing is as old as mankind itself. The earliest recorded users

Nature's treasure chest

The medical evidence is still sketchy, but here are herbal remedies that have shown promise.

CAYENNE AND OTHER PEPPERS

Peppers contain a strong analgesic and

Fresh ginger can enhance your food and your life

anti-inflammatory agent known as capsaicin. This compound blocks a chemical in the body that acts as a pain signal. You can find capsaicin in many commercial creams and ointments for arthritis pain. Typical dosage for a cream containing 0.25–0.75% capsaicin is a single daily application. Some people might experience a slight burning of the skin with capsaicin use.

FLAX

The linoleic acid found in flaxseed oil may also be beneficial for arthritis because it alters how the body breaks down postaglandins, chemicals involved in inflammation. Typical dosage is 2 tablespoons of oil per day in food, either in salad dressings or on top of cereals.

GINGER

This root has traditionally been used in India to treat arthritis. Components of ginger such as gingerol can inhibit the production of the prostaglandins. People with diabetes or heart problems should be cautious of a dose of greater than 500 mg per day in capsule form or a half to one teaspoon of fresh ground root.

DEVIL'S CLAW

This herb from Africa has traditionally been used for most types of arthritis. The tubers contain a group of chemicals called iridoids that have anti-inflammatory effects, although the clinical evidence is far from conclusive. One clinical study showed patients with arthritis reported less pain when taking one 500 mg tablet of devil's claw three times a day. Other studies, however, conclude that it provides no relief for arthritis.

were the ancient Egyptians, Greeks, Romans, Chinese, and, more recently, the native American Indians. Up to 70% of the world's population still relies on this form of therapy.

How does herbal medicine work?

Unlike modern medicine, which isolates, refines, and even synthesizes a plant's therapeutic properties, medical herbalists use the whole plant. Professionally, the practice is known as phytotherapy—from the Greek words phyton meaning plant, and therapeuein, to take care of, to heal.

Expert opinion

"The herbal approach to inflammatory and degenerative joint conditions can yield excellent results," claims Trudy Norris, a practising medical herbalist and communications officer for the National Institute of Medical Herbalists (NIMH). "Practitioners approach each case individually, noting current health status, past medical history, and current medication. They consider diet, circulation, post- or pre-menopausal status, physical trauma, excessive stress, digestion, food, or environmental intolerance/allergy. The herbalist may treat a whole range of arthritic complaints including osteo- and rheumatoid arthritis and psoriatic arthritis. People of all ages are treated, including children. The practitioner combines herbs that complement and enhance each others' actions. Practitioners normally see patients monthly to evaluate progress in overall health as well as judging any reduction in pain and swelling and improved mobility."

Open wide

The herbs that Norris uses most frequently for arthritis are white willow bark and meadowsweet (Salix alba and Filipendula ulmaria). Hawthorn is also used to improve circulation, and wild yam is believed to be a good anti-inflammatory. Oats, lavender, and valerian are all recommended to help the nervous system. Herbs can be dispensed in a number of forms including tinctures, fluid extracts, teas, and tablets, or a topical cream, embrocation or plaster.

Norris advises: "People should consult a qualified practitioner or visit a reputable outlet like a health store or pharmacy. They should also be prepared to give the preparation some time to work. One over-the-counter preparation I would recommend trying is devil's claw."

HOMEOPATHY

Homeopathy is a science that constantly divides medical opinion. It was pioneered by Samuel Hahneman in Germany in the late 1700s and is based on the theory that "like cures like." A highly diluted form of the original material is violently shaken in alcohol thousands of times. Homeopaths believe that the remedies eventually carry the healing energy imprint of the original substance. The theory is that this influences the energy imbalance responsible for the patient's symptoms.

Expert opinion

Dr Neil Slade, a homeopath practising in London, treats many patients with arthritis. In fact, he says: "More and more, we are becoming the first port of call. There has been

HOMEOPATHY CASE STUDY

Helena, aged 76, has suffered from a progressive curvature of the spine due to osteoporosis and osteoarthritis of the hips and lumbar spine. Recently she developed severe pain in her lower back and left hip, which extended down her groin and inner thigh. The pain was severe enough to confine her to bed and she needed the use of two sticks and the support of her husband to walk to the bathroom. Strong painkillers prescribed by her GP offered no relief, and the pain was still as severe two weeks later.

Slade started Helena on a remedy called Zeel-T, belonging to "complex homeopathy". He prescribed one tablet three times daily and Zeel-T cream massaged into her groin and thigh twice daily. "She decided to abandon her painkillers and within four days she was able to walk downstairs for the first time in two weeks, after 10 days she was able to go out for lunch. She still has some degree of pain in the hip joint but is improving daily and is fully mobile without the use of her walking sticks."

an historic trend for sufferers to take conventional treatment as their primary care and come on to complementary therapy afterwards. But we're turning that on its head. We check their total health profile including their diet, because some studies have shown a correlation between rheumatoid arthritis and an imbalance of bacteria in the gut, so we look at prescribing a probiotic."

Can I buy remedies over the counter?

No two patients will present with the same degree of symptoms, but the remedies most prescribed by Slade are Rhus tox, Bryonia and Ruta. "These can be bought over the counter as single remedies or in combination form. Sadly, we are yet to be regulated, so anyone can get hold of remedies and self-prescribe. All homeopathic remedies are available from homeopathic pharmacies, but only certain ones can be purchased from outlets such as Boots and Holland and Barrett." Dr Slade recommends two homeopathic pharmacies, Ainsworths (**www.ainsworths.com**) and Helios (**www.helios.co.uk**)—both have a comprehensive advice service.

Open wide

It may take a few days for the remedy to start working and symptoms may actually worsen at first. Take nothing orally 30 minutes before and after the remedy. Avoid coffee, mints, and menthol/eucalyptus. Suck the tablet like a boiled sweet until it has dissolved. Store remedies in a cool, dark place away from strong-smelling things, which may antidote or reduce the effect of the remedy.

HEALING HANDS
Acupuncture

This system of healing has been practised in China and other Eastern countries for thousands of years. Its roots lie in traditional Chinese medicine, which believes that our health depends on the body's motivating energy, called Qi (pronounced "chee"), running in a smooth and balanced way through a series of channels (meridians) through the skin. When the flow of Qi is put out of balance, illness results. Acupuncture involves inserting fine needles into specific

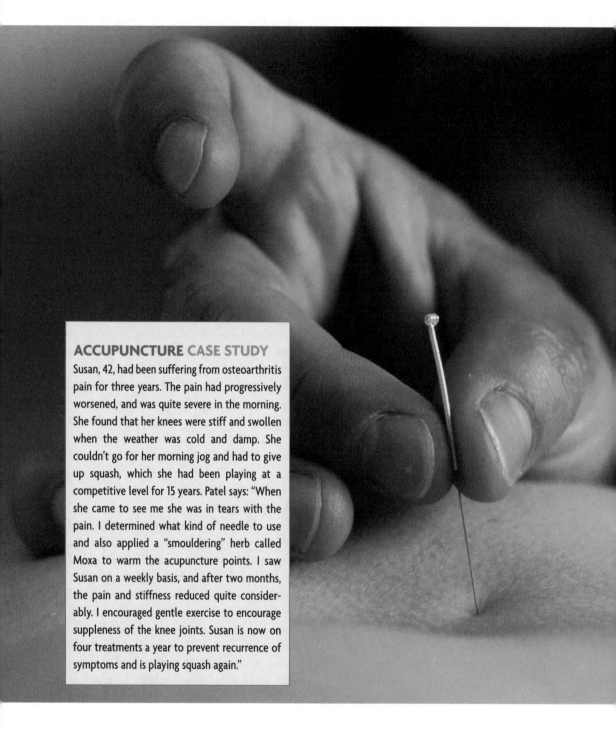

ACCUPUNCTURE CASE STUDY

Susan, 42, had been suffering from osteoarthritis pain for three years. The pain had progressively worsened, and was quite severe in the morning. She found that her knees were stiff and swollen when the weather was cold and damp. She couldn't go for her morning jog and had to give up squash, which she had been playing at a competitive level for 15 years. Patel says: "When she came to see me she was in tears with the pain. I determined what kind of needle to use and also applied a "smouldering" herb called Moxa to warm the acupuncture points. I saw Susan on a weekly basis, and after two months, the pain and stiffness reduced quite considerably. I encouraged gentle exercise to encourage suppleness of the knee joints. Susan is now on four treatments a year to prevent recurrence of symptoms and is playing squash again."

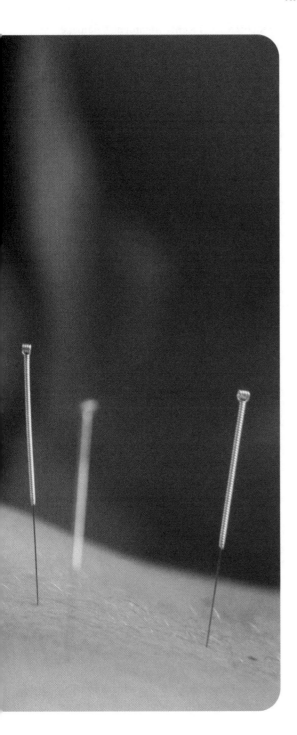

points in the body to correct the imbalance—it's a viable option for people with arthritis because although the process is invasive, it is not painful in the way you'd expect.

Expert Opinion

Acupuncturist Archna Patel, a member of the British Acupuncture Council says that an imbalance can be created by poor nutrition, weather conditions, hereditary factors, infections, trauma, incorrect joint alignment, and muscular tension. All these issues should be taken into consideration when you go for a consultation with an acupuncturist. Osteoarthritis, she says, is easier to treat than RA as it has less underlying complications. "How the fine needles are inserted depends on the patient's condition. If a knee joint is hot and inflamed, then we treat the less affected knee."

CHIROPRACTIC

Chiropractic treatment was first practised in the late 19th century. It is based on the theory that the vertebrae in your spine can become malaligned (subluxated)—placing pressure on the nerves, which impacts on various body parts and systems, and in turn compromises the body's ability to work at its optimum.

Expert opinion

Dr David Thomas trained and qualified as a chiropractor after treatment transformed his life following a back injury. His advice is: "Get your spine checked from cradle to grave. Chiropractic can help, even resolve, problems of pain in the back and the joints. But people need to use chiropractic treatment on a regular basis for it to become preventative. By the time the pain manifests, arthritis has taken root."

Dr Thomas uses a simple analogy—the Leaning Tower of Pisa. "When the body adapts to outside influences such as injury, it compensates by deviating to left or right, creating an inherent asymmetry. Unchecked, it could all come tumbling down." Chiropractic treatment, he says, explains why this has happened and uses a variety of techniques to "unwind" it. David does gentle manipulation techniques that are also suitable for older people with arthritic symptoms. He also looks thoroughly at dietary issues to identify food intolerances or nutritional deficiency.

Caution

Chiropractic techniques can be quite vigorous and are not suitable for people suffering from acute inflammation or infection, severe osteoporosis, recent ligament damage, fractures, or chronic circulatory problems. This is also a therapy that should be avoided by anyone with limited spinal mobility due to Ankylosing Spondylytis.

REFLEXOLOGY

Reflexology applies varying degrees of pressure to different parts of the body to promote health and well-being. It suggests that each part of the body is connected by "reflex zones" or "pathways" that end in the soles of the feet, palms of the hands, ears, tongue, and head. The belief is that tension, congestion, or some other imbalance will affect an entire zone, and that it is possible to treat one part of the zone to affect another part of the body.

Expert opinion

Terry Cullen is vice chair of the British Complementary Medicine Association (BCMA) and a practising reflexologist: "Reflexology is well established as a means of achieving appreciable relief from pain and stiffness in arthritic joints. As part of a holistic approach, the therapist will consider diet, supplementation, and water intake. Reflexology is effective at reducing inflammation and encouraging fluid circulation. If the patient drinks enough water, the synovial fluid in the joints should increase."

OTHER THERAPIES

Alexander Technique

The Alexander technique was developed a century ago by Australian actor Frederick Matthias Alexander to improve his voice. The principle behind the technique is that poor

CHIROPRACTIC CASE STUDY

Linda, 60, had a history of chronic back problems and required surgery on two occasions. She was in a lot of pain, and as a result of surgery had lost the feeling in her right leg. She also had neck problems. She'd had conventional treatment, "but," says Dr Thomas, "she just wasn't being properly attended to. We took the holistic approach, including a test for water retention and food intolerance. As well as using a number of chiropractic treatments, we cut several foods from her diet and prescribed a probiotic and mineral and herbal supplement. She is now feeling eminently better and coping generally with life."

posture, malco-ordination, and muscle tension inhibit the body's ability to function to the best of its ability, be it on stage, in a sporting context, or in normal day-to-day activities.

Alexander technique teachers help you become more body-aware and mentally alert, to carry yourself properly, and be better co-ordinated. By doing so, they believe you can help yourself relieve stress, sleep problems, and chronic pain.

Massage

There are many sorts of massage, but all are based on the principle that hands-on manipulation of soft tissue—muscles, connective tissues, tendons, and ligaments—can have therapeutic effects by speeding up the elimination of toxins in the body.

By rhythmically kneading soft tissue, masseurs can help reduce tension and fatigue, improve circulation and so reduce pain. Massage can be gentle and relaxing, or vigorous. Because arthritis sufferers have sensitive joints, practitioners will use specially-tailored gentle techniques to help alleviate pain and stiffness, particularly around the joints.

Osteopathy

Osteopaths focus on the musculoskeletal system—the joints, muscles, and bones—which they believe are vital to the healthy functioning of the entire body. Occasionally, techniques such as ultrasound are used, but the primary method of osteopathy is for the practitioner to use his or her hands to diagnose and treat any existing problems, and to promote general well-being by re-aligning the spine. There is also emphasis on diet, posture,

and exercise. Osteopaths believe that gentle manipulation and correct alignment help the body to heal itself.

Cautionary Notes

As many complemtary therapies are unproven, and their practitioners unregulated, it's well worth remembering these common-sense guidelines before trying a new therapy.

Ask your GP whether they think that the complementary treatment you're considering will work for you, and whether it will react with your other treatments. Always tell your GP or rheumatologist about everything you are trying or taking.

Ask your complementary medicine practitioner if they can put you in touch with other people with a similar condition to yours

Manipulating posture can help bring healing

that they've treated. Check and double check qualifications, training, and insurance.

Warning Signs

A large number of complementary medicine practitioners are highly trained and have high standards of professional ethics and practice, but some do not. Your GP may be able to recommend a reputable practitioner, but if they can't, look out for:

Miracle cures

Many treatments will help arthritis, but arthritis cannot be "cured." A reputable complementary health practitioner—like a good doctor—will never promise a cure.

Reduced drugs

Never stop or reduce your prescription medication unless your rheumatologist or GP tells you to. Stopping some medications can lead to flare-ups, and can be dangerous.

Extreme diets

Good, balanced nutrition is a key to arthritis treatment, so be wary of any practitioner that involves eliminating a large number of foods.

Advance payment

Walk away from anyone who asks for large sums of cash before treatment.

Proof

Don't accept treatment from anyone who can show you no evidence of his or her training.

Secrecy

Avoid anyone who tells you not to tell your doctor that you're receiving treatment from them.

USEFUL CONTACTS

British Complementary Medicine Association (BCMA)
PO Box 1522
Bournemouth
BH8 OWG
Tel: 0845 345 5977
www.bcma.co.uk

Prince of Wales's Foundation for Integrated Health
12 Chillingworth Road
London N7 8QJ
Tel: 020 7619 6140
www.fihealth.org.uk
(Just launched a one-stop guide to CAM for consumers)

National Institute of Medical Herbalists
56 Longbrook Street
Exeter EX4 6AH
Tel: 01392 426022
www.nimh.org.uk

British Herbal Medicine Association (BHMA)
1 Wickham Road
Boscombe
Bournemouth
Dorset BH7 6JX
Tel: 01202 433691
www.bhma.info

Health Supplements Information Service (HSIS)
Bury House
126-128 Bury Road

London SW7 4ET
Tel: 020 7370 2233
www.hsis.org

British Acupuncture Council
63 Jeddo Road
London W12 9HQ
Tel: 020 8735 0400
www.acupuncture.org.uk

British Medical Acupuncture Society
BMAS House
3 Winnington Court
Northwich
Cheshire CW8 1AQ
Tel: 01606 786782
www.medical-acupuncture.co.uk

British Holistic Medical Association
59 Lansdown Place
Hove, East Sussex BN3 1FL
Tel: 01273 725951
www.bhma.org

**British Homeopathic
Association**
Hahnemann House
29 Park Street West
Luton LU1 3BE
Tel: 0870 444 3950
www.trusthomeopathy.org

**The Chartered Society of
Physiotherapy**
14 Bedford Row
London WC1R 4ED

Tel: 020 7306 6666
www.csp.org.uk

British Reflexology Association
Monks Orchard
Whitbourne
Worcester WR6 5RB
Tel: 01886 821207
www.britreflex.co.uk

Institute for Complementary Medicine
PO Box 194
London SE16 7QZ
Tel: 020 7237 5165
www.icmedicine.co.uk

International Federation of Aromatherapy
182 Chiswick High Road
London W4 1PP
Tel: 020 8742 2605
www.ifaroma.org

National Rheumatoid Arthritis Society
Briarwood House
11 College Avenue
Maidenhead
Berkshire SL6 6AR
Tel: 01628 670606
www.rheumatoid.org.uk

Society of Teachers of the Alexander Technique
1st Floor, Linton House
39-51 Highgate Road
London NW5 1RS
Tel: 0845 230 7828
www.stat.org.uk

strong nutrition for strong joints

What you eat can have a positive—or negative—effect on your arthritis

CHAPTER 8

The Ultimate Weight Loss Diet

Take off pounds for good—and ease your arthritis—
with this never-feel-hungry plan

Arthritis sufferers have more to gain than most from losing weight. By literally taking weight off those sore joints, you can reduce the pain as well as look better.

But what's the secret of losing weight and keeping it off? Can you change your diet without condemning yourself to constant hunger, or must shedding pounds always be a triumph of willpower over appetite?

Here's the answer—the Ultimate Weight Loss Diet. A complete nutrition plan, including all the foods proven to promote lasting weight loss, while keeping

The perfect diet for lasting weight loss

hunger at bay.

It's not a crash diet. The Ultimate Weight Loss Diet is based on a daily energy requirement of around 1,500 calories per day. For most people that will result in gradual, sustainable weight loss.

By dividing this daily calorie allowance into six mini-meals of 250 calories, you'll avoid the hunger pangs and energy dips that make dieting so difficult for many people. You'll also train your body to burn calories more efficiently—a vital key to weight loss.

If 1,500 calories isn't enough for you, the Ultimate Weight Loss Diet is flexible—simply double the portions in one or more of your mini-meals.

Over the last two decades, we have learned an enormous amount about how diet impacts arthritis, in both positive and negative ways. The dietary recommendations for controlling the symptoms of arthritis are pretty much the same whether you have osteoarthritis or rheumatoid arthritis.

The most important thing about this diet is that it's nutritionally correct—not only does it provide all the major nutrients you need for good health—it can play an active long-term role in reducing the risk of high blood pressure, stroke, cancer, diabetes, osteoporosis, cataracts, obesity, asthma, diverticulitis, depression, and even PMS.

Place the emphasis on fruit and veg when you shop

But first...

Let's take a look at what certain nutrients can do to help the type of arthritis you have.

The Arthritis Food Guide Pyramid is, in many ways, similar to a normal healthy eating plan. But there are also several significant differences. Grains no longer make up the dietary base on which everything else rests. Water does. Fruits and vegetables figure more prominently than grains, too. And among protein-rich foods, fish, beans, and soya foods become more important than beef and poultry.

Water moisturizes and gives structural support to the joints and other tissues. It carries nutrients and oxygen to the joints as well as to the rest of the body through the blood and lymphatic systems. In addition, it plays a crucial role in maintaining body temperature: the heat released when we lose water via evaporation of perspiration helps cool down the body.

Because the thirst sensation does not always kick in when it should, we advise everyone to drink at least 8 cups of fluid a day, preferably water. Juices and (non-caffeinated) fizzy drinks will take care of your fluid needs, but at a great calorific expense. And caffeinated beverages, including coffee, tea, and many fizzy drinks, are diuretics, which means they tend to draw water from you.

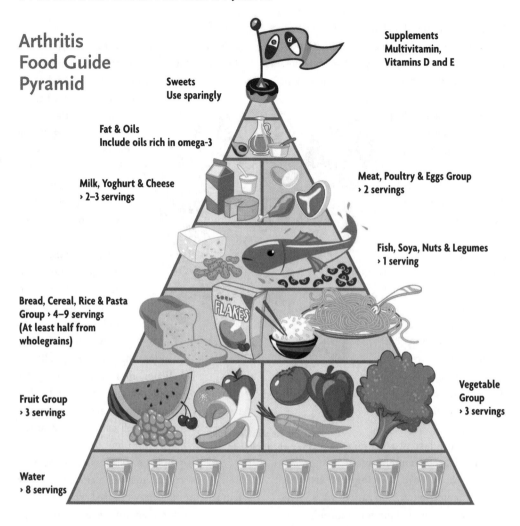

Arthritis Food Guide Pyramid

Supplements
Multivitamin,
Vitamins D and E

Sweets
Use sparingly

Fat & Oils
Include oils rich in omega-3

Milk, Yoghurt & Cheese
› 2–3 servings

Meat, Poultry & Eggs Group
› 2 servings

Fish, Soya, Nuts & Legumes
› 1 serving

Bread, Cereal, Rice & Pasta
Group › 4–9 servings
(At least half from
wholegrains)

Fruit Group
› 3 servings

Vegetable
Group
› 3 servings

Water
› 8 servings

Fish oil and Rheumatoid Arthritis

Fish oils, which are rich in omega-3 fatty acids, lead to the creation of anti-inflammatory prostaglandins. The two most important types of fish oil are eicosapentaenoic acid (EPA) and docosahexaenoic acid (DHA). These oils are found in high concentrations in cold-water fish such as salmon and mackerel.

In one analysis of nine different research projects, fish oil capsules were found to reduce tenderness in three different joints and to reduce morning stiffness as well. The relief was modest, but when the pain is bad enough to keep you from doing the things you like, "modest" is pretty good.

A Danish study in which people with rheumatoid arthritis were put on a specialized diet that included an average of 100 g of fish

Healthy Weight Loss Tricks

Here are two tips that will help keep you on track with the Ultimate Weight Loss Diet and ensure you're getting optimum nutrition.

STICK TO A FAT BUDGET

Try to stay within a healthy fat budget—25% of calories from fat. First, find the maximum fat allowance for your calorie level on this chart.

MAXIMUM FAT ALLOWANCE

Calories	Grams of Fat
1,250	35
1,500	42
1,750	49
2,000	56
2,250	63

Once you know your fat budget, see whether you're staying within the bounds by adding up the grams of fat for all the food that you eat in a day. Almost all food labels will tell you the grams of total fat in a serving. The Ultimate Weight Loss Diet is designed to give approximately 42 g of fat, the healthy limit for a 1,500-calorie-per-day diet.

Remember: a diet low in saturated fat can help ease arthritis pain in addition to helping you lose weight. Try to get most of your fat from healthier, inflammation-reducing olive and rapeseed oils (or salad dressings made from them), margarine, nuts, and fish.

TAKE SOME NUTRITION INSURANCE

The Ultimate Weight Loss Diet will provide your body with optimum nutrition, but few of us eat perfectly every day, and that's where supplements can help. Buying a few health-promoting supplements and taking them regularly will help keep your body stocked with disease- and arthritis-fighting nutrients.

Here's what you should take: a multivitamin/ mineral supplement, and 100 to 500 mg of vitamin C. On days when you eat only two calcium-rich foods, take 500 mg of calcium if you're under 50; take 1,000 mg calcium (divided into two doses of 500 mg each) if you're 50 or older.

Take multivitamins to supplement your diet

Know When to Take Calcium

Take calcium carbonate with meals; you can take calcium citrate on an empty stomach. For best absorption, don't take more than 500 mg at one time.

every day experienced a significant decrease in morning stiffness, swollen joints, and pain in general, after following the regimen for 6 months. They also ended up spending less money on medications to reduce pain and inflammation.

Freshen up your diet with raw vegetables

Fresh produce takes on new prominence

Fruits and vegetables are the only food groups that contain substantial amounts of vitamin C, vitamin A, and folate—which are all nutrients that people with osteoarthritis and rheumatoid arthritis need more of than the average person.

While the Reference Nutrient Intake (RNI) of vitamin C is 40 milligrams, we suggest 200 milligrams. In cases of osteoarthritis, vitamin C at this level appears to help reduce pain. And those with rheumatoid arthritis apparently "use up" much more vitamin C than others, and therefore require a much greater supply. Fortunately, if you are eating a daily minimum of 3 fruits and 3 vegetables for a total of at least 6 servings of produce (which will also help with any weight-control effort), it's fairly easy to reach the 200-milligram mark.

Note that some of the sources of both vitamin C, betacarotene and vitamin A are green leafy vegetables, such as broccoli, Brussels sprouts, spinach and kale. Whatever you do, DON'T take single-nutrient beta-carotene pills, as large doses of beta-carotene have been found to be harmful for some groups of people.

Go for grains

We recommend that you choose wholegrains such as wholegrain breads and breakfast cereals, oatmeal and brown rice, along with some lesser-utilized wholegrains such as bulgar wheat and barley. Wholegrains, as opposed to refined grains (such as those in white bread, spaghetti, and white rice), contain fibre, which most of us do not get enough of. In Britain, we typically consume about 10–15 grams of fibre daily, when the target should be 18 grams.

Points on protein

Protein is an essential nutrient. The protein in our diet supplies amino acids—the building blocks for structural components in the body (muscles, cartilage, and bone).

One of our recommendations is to eat more cold-water fish, the most important protein in your diet if you have arthritis. Cold-water species are the only rich source of the two most effective omega-3 fatty acids (EPA and DHA) that are so important in fighting the inflammatory process of arthritis. They are also low in the pro-inflammatory omega-6 oils. Eating 4 servings of fish a week should guarantee the recommended consumption level of the two omega-3 fatty acids found only in fish. You can average out your intake over the course of a week.

Meats (beef, chicken, and pork), on the other hand, have virtually no EPA or DHA and very little other omega-3s, but they have significantly more omega-6s, -9s, and saturated fat.

Aside from adding fish to the diet, choosing more vegetable proteins—tofu (bean curd), beans, nuts, and seeds—will also boost your intake of omega-3s.

Sample Menu

BREAKFAST
1/2 wholewheat muffin
1 teaspoon margarine
1 poached or hard-boiled egg
1 pear

MID-MORNING SNACK
120 g low-fat vanilla yoghurt
50 g luxury muesli

LUNCH
2 slices wholewheat bread
50 g reduced-fat mozzarella cheese
1 roasted pepper (packed in water)
basil leaves

MID-AFTERNOON SNACK
50 g houmous
6-8 cucumber slices

DINNER
75 g poached salmon
150 g brown rice
100 g tomatoes
100 g steamed kale

EVENING SNACK
125 ml calcium-fortified orange juice
1 banana

DAY'S TOTAL =
Calories: 1,506; **Fat:** 38 g; **Sat fat:** 10 g
Fibre: 21 g; **Sodium:** 1,337 mg

How Big Is a Serving?

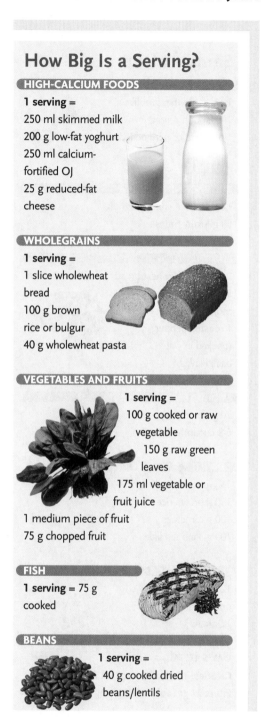

HIGH-CALCIUM FOODS

1 serving =
250 ml skimmed milk
200 g low-fat yoghurt
250 ml calcium-
fortified OJ
25 g reduced-fat
cheese

WHOLEGRAINS

1 serving =
1 slice wholewheat
bread
100 g brown
rice or bulgur
40 g wholewheat pasta

VEGETABLES AND FRUITS

1 serving =
100 g cooked or raw
vegetable
150 g raw green
leaves
175 ml vegetable or
fruit juice
1 medium piece of fruit
75 g chopped fruit

FISH

1 serving = 75 g
cooked

BEANS

1 serving =
40 g cooked dried
beans/lentils

Dairy dos and don'ts

Two to 3 servings of dairy foods a day are important to the health of your bones, which are so integrally involved in joint function.

Try to make as many dairy choices as possible low-fat. If dairy is not for you, there are options that can help fill the void. Soya milk is widely available today, and many brands come fortified with vitamin D and calcium (check labels).

Supplements as Insurance

Take a multivitamin to make sure your nutritional bases are always covered.

We cannot definitively recommend that you take supplemental doses of vitamin E. However, if you want to try it, we think it may be helpful. Make sure to stick to 400 milligrams a day.

Every Day:
MORE CALCIUM
WHY

There is strong evidence that calcium plays a part in reducing body fat—in addition to its better-known role in forming and maintaining healthy bones.

A group of women who ate at least 1,000 mg of calcium a day, along with a diet of no more than 1,900 calories daily, lost more weight—as much as 6 lb more during a 2-year study—than women who ate less calcium.

This may be because calcium suppresses hormones involved in fat production, while promoting fat breakdown.

If you are 50 or older, or have low bone density, you should get 1,500 mg of calcium daily. If you're younger than 50, aim for 1,000mg.

You probably already know that calcium is important for strong bones and helps prevent osteoporosis. Arthritis sufferers should also know that milk—the leading source of calcium for most people—is rich in vitamin D, which helps ease arthritis.

Research has also shown possible links between calcium and reduced risk of colon cancer, high blood pressure, and PMS.

HOW

➤ Obvious healthy high-calcium dairy food choices include skimmed milk, low-fat yoghurt, and reduced-fat cheese.

➤ Other good ideas are orange and grapefruit juices, and soya milk that has been fortified with calcium. To equal the calcium found in milk, look for at least 30% of the RNI (700 mg/day) for calcium per serving.

➤ If you're lactose-intolerant, look for lactose-free dairy products.

➤ Besides dairy products, load up on calcium-rich foods such as tofu, sardines, and spinach.

Calcium-rich foods

Milk (including skimmed milk)
Yoghurt (including low-fat)
Cheese
Fortified soya milk
Bean curd (tofu)
Sardines
Spinach
Dried beans and peas
Broccoli
Rhubarb

MORE WHOLEGRAINS
WHY

Wholegrains mean fibre—your best friend when it comes to losing weight. Not only does fibre fill you up quickly with fewer calories, but it even eliminates some of the calories you eat! High-fibre food moves through your digestive system so quickly that some of its fat content is never absorbed.

Wholegrains have been shown to lower rates of heart disease, stroke, diabetes, and cancer.

These days, most of the carbohydrate-rich, white flour-based foods you're used to are available in wholegrain equivalents—though you may have to search a little for some! It's worth it, though. To your body, refined white flour is the same thing as sugar, making a diet high in white-flour foods the same as a high-sugar diet.

Your target should be to eat 18 g of fibre a day. That will mean you absorb up to 120 fewer calories daily—or lose 30 lb weight in a year.

HOW

➤ Make sure you're getting true wholegrain products. Look for the word "whole" on the ingredients list.

➤ Look for bread that contains at least 2 g of fibre per slice and for breakfast cereals that contain at least 3 g per serving.

➤ Switch from refined products such as Ritz crackers and regular spaghetti to wholegrain products such as wholewheat crackers and wholewheat spaghetti.

➤ Add barley to soups.

➤ Use bulgar wheat in your favourite coleslaw recipe.

➤ Eat porridge for breakfast.

MORE VEGETABLES AND FRUIT
WHY

Vegetables and fruits are the foundation of the Ultimate Weight Loss Diet—as opposed to grains, the foundation of the traditional Food Guide Pyramid. Eat up to nine servings of a variety of fruits and vegetables every day.

The beauty of fruits and vegetables is that, in addition to helping you lose weight, they can also prolong your life. There is a huge weight of evidence to suggest that they are also linked with reduced incidence of cancer, heart disease, diabetes, and osteoporosis. For the arthritis sufferer there is the added benefit of high levels of antioxidants such as vitamins A, C, and E— all of which can ease arthritis.

The typical British diet includes just four servings of fruit and vegetables per day, whereas experts recommend between five and nine servings daily. The Ultimate Weight Loss Diet makes every meal and snack a fruit or vegetable opportunity.

Mix a salad for your veg allowance

HOW

➤ Add sliced fruit to your breakfast cereal— and anything else you can think of.

➤ Drink fruit or vegetable juice instead of fizzy drinks.

➤ Eat whole fruit, such as apples, or raw vegetables, such as cauliflower, as snacks instead of sweets.

➤ Accompany lunch or dinner with a mixed salad.

➤ Put lettuce, tomato, onions, sliced cucumbers, broccoli, and other vegetables in your sandwiches.

➤ Add extra vegetables to stir-fries, sauces, and casseroles.

➤ Use time-saving frozen and canned vegetables and fruits, which provide as much nutrition as fresh produce.

MORE WATER

8 glasses a day, plus at least one cup of tea

WHY

Every cell in your body needs water to function, and drinking lots of water helps you feel full. Big water drinkers appear to get less colon and bladder cancers.

In addition, every cup of tea provides a strong infusion of antioxidants that help keep your blood from clotting too easily (which in turn may thwart heart attacks) and that may help lower your risk of cancer and rheumatoid arthritis.

HOW

➤ To encourage yourself to drink more water, purchase a large water bottle and put a plastic straw in it. Keep it filled with water, and sip from it throughout the day.

➤ If you don't like the taste of water, jazz it up with a shot of fruit juice or a squeeze or two of fresh lemon or lime.

➤ Both green and black teas contain powerful antioxidants. So drink whichever one you prefer.

Vitamins for Osteoarthritis

VITAMIN C

In the Framingham Heart Study in the USA, researchers found that the progression of osteoarthritis was reduced by more than half in the people who consumed an average of at least 152 milligrams of vitamin C a day. Vitamin C is thought to help reduce pain for two reasons. Firstly, it is important in the formation of collagen and proteoglycans—the major components of cartilage. Secondly, it's an antioxidant nutrient that can quench free radicals. Free radicals—highly reactive and unstable compounds produced in the body—can rip through cartilage

like bullets, damaging its structure. As the damage occurs, there's inflammation at the joint. That's where vitamin C is believed to be beneficial; it's thought to neutralize free radicals before they have a chance to destroy cartilage.

VITAMIN D

Osteoarthritis damages not just the cartilage but also the underlying bones. That's a problem because bones help maintain joint stability. Bones and cartilage "communicate" with each other to allow for a healthy joint. So any bone abnormalities resulting from osteoarthritis can contribute to loss of mobility. The way vitamin D comes into play here is that it's crucial for bone strength and structure.

BETA-CAROTENE AND VITAMIN E

The case for beta-carotene and vitamin E, both antioxidants, is not as strong as it is for vitamins C or D. The Framingham researchers did find that people with osteoarthritis of the knee who consumed more than 5.4 mcg of beta-carotene a day (an amount easily obtained from a diet rich in fruits and vegetables) were at reduced risk of disease progression compared with people whose daily consumption was less than 3 mcg. They were also much less likely to suffer knee pain later on.

As for vitamin E, people with knee arthritis in the Framingham trial who consumed 6–11 milligrams of vitamin E daily were 60 per cent less likely over a 10-year period to experience disease progression than those who took in only 2–5 milligrams.

Try These Low-Calorie Snacks

Some satisfying snacks that contain only about 160 calories each:

15 g homemade popcorn and 225 ml of juice

3 medium chocolate chip biscuits

Every Week
MORE FISH

4 servings per week

WHY

The protein in fish is a great hunger-stopper—and it helps build healthy muscles that burn lots of calories. "And protein is important for promoting satiety—the feeling of fullness you look for from a meal," says biomedical researcher Dr Michael Hamilton. In addition to satisfying your hunger, fish is rich in omega-3 fatty acids, which are known to reduce the inflammation of rheumatoid arthritis.

HOW

➤ To get the most omega-3s, choose salmon, tuna canned in water, rainbow trout, anchovies, herring, sardines, and mackerel.

➤ Choose water-packed tuna with the highest fat content. Fat can range from 0.5 to 5 g per serving. The more total fat, the more omega-3s.

➤ Most salmon, including the farm-raised kind, is rich in omega-3s. The exception is smoked salmon, which loses most of its fat, including omega-3s.

MORE BEANS

5 servings per week

WHY

As we already mentioned, fibre can help you lose weight by making you feel full and by ushering calories out of your body. And beans

Salmon contains plenty of protein and omega-3 oils

are the highest-fibre foods you can find, with the single exception of breakfast cereals made with wheat bran. Diets high in fibre are linked to less cancer, heart disease, diabetes, stroke, and even ulcers. Beans are especially high in soluble fibre, which lowers cholesterol levels, and folate, which lowers levels of yet another risk factor for heart disease—homocysteine.

HOW

➤ Just add beans to omelettes, pizzas and anything else you fancy. They go well with sweetcorn, peppers, tomato, and spring onions.

➤ Use houmous on everything, from sandwiches to salads.

➤ Combine chickpeas and kidney beans with tomatoes, cucumber, spring onions, garlic, feta cheese, and chopped, fresh mint for a delicious salad.

➤ To reduce sodium in canned beans by about one-third, rinse off the canning liquid before using. Or look for canned beans with no added sodium.

Help yourself

These choices are up to you with The Ultimate Weight Loss Diet.

MEAT

You'll get enough protein on The Ultimate Weight Loss Diet without adding meat, and studies consistently link vegetarian diets to better health and lower weight, perhaps partly because diets low in meat are lower in saturated fat. Also, meat may be associated with the body's inflammatory response and could trigger gout attacks. But if you want, you can choose up to 75 g (the size of a deck of cards) of meat or poultry per day.

Get Fibre from Fruit

Many fruits are good sources of fibre as well as vitamins. Here is the fibre content of some popular varieties. Remember, your target is at least 25 g of fibre a day.

FRUIT	SERVING SIZE	FIBRE (G)
Red raspberries	125 g	11.0
Guava	165 g	9.0
Papaya	1 med	5.5
Blueberries	145 g	3.9
Apple	1 med	3.7
Strawberries (whole)	150 g	3.3
Orange	1 med	3.1
Mango	165 g	3.0
Banana	1 med	2.8
Kiwi fruit	1 med	2.6
Red grapes	160 g	1.5
Pink grapefruit	1/2 med	1.4

EGGS

Up to 7 eggs a week is okay, or up to 4 if you have diabetes or high cholesterol, or are overweight.

ALCOHOL

Women should limit alcohol to one drink a day. Men should limit their alcohol intake to two drinks a day, although alcohol can be a trigger for some forms of arthritis. Studies show that moderate alcohol consumption, especially of red wine, lowers the risk of heart disease. But it also slightly raises the risk of breast cancer.

CHAPTER 9

Beat Arthritis— Naturally!

Some natural remedies can ease the pain of arthritis while others are useless. Here's how to tell the difference

Shark Cartilage. Fish Oil. Gamma linolenic acid (GLA). You've undoubtedly heard of them because they're all touted to help—if not "cure"—arthritis. But do they work?

As you probably suspect, some do and some don't (although nothing can completely cure arthritis). We spend millions of pounds every year on unproven, and ineffective, arthritis remedies. But you don't have to do that. This guide will help you choose the right natural remedy to ease your pain, without wasting your money. After you've read our supplement review, follow our "Shop smart" advice on page 77 to make sure that you get your money's worth at the health shop!

There's nothing fishy about omega-3 fatty acids

THE GOOD REMEDIES
Green Tea

The claim: Polyphenols in green tea have been shown to reduce inflammation, one of the painful and debilitating symptoms of Rheumatoid Arthritis (RA).

The proof: Mice given green tea extract had much lower rates of arthritis than mice not given the extract. Human trials are needed, but as green tea is totally safe, it may be worth a try anyway.

Suggested dose: Three to four cups a day, which is equivalent to 600 to 800 mg of polyphenols. It's also available in decaffeinated and flavoured versions, or as capsules. If you buy decaf, make sure it has been decaffeinated using water and carbon dioxide—a process called effervescence—or the polyphenols will be destroyed. If the label doesn't specify, ask the manufacturer. Don't forget that milk may interfere with the polyphenol's action, so drink green tea plain.

Fish Oil

The claim: The omega-3 fatty acids in fish oil—eicosapentaenoic acid (EPA) and docosahexaenoic acid (DHA)—may ease RA symptoms by providing anti-inflammatory building blocks.

The proof: Many studies have shown that fish oil helps the inflammation and accompanying pain of RA. It may reduce the need for NSAIDs such as ibuprofen. It

Antioxidants can help too

Need another reason to get your five fruit and veg a day? How about this: some studies have shown that the antioxidants in fruit and vegetables may protect joints —especially knees—from the ravages of osteoarthritis. Here are some of the studies' findings:

➤ People with high intakes of vitamin C and beta-carotene had a reduced risk of knee pain and disease progression.

➤ Certain antioxidants (including lutein and lycopene) were associated with a lower risk of knee OA.

➤ The evidence is far from conclusive but in some controlled studies, vitamin E eased arthritis pain better than a placebo or NSAIDs.

To make certain that you are getting enough beta-carotene, lutein, lycopene, and vitamin C, eat plenty of carrots, sweet potatoes, broccoli, spinach, tomatoes, oranges, kiwi fruit, and strawberries. Try to increase your fruit and veg intake to nine servings a day if you can.

Eat oranges to save your knees

The healing power of snakes

Here's a traditional Chinese treatment for arthritis. Add 100 snakes to 5 litres of wine and some herbs. Leave to mellow for three months, then drink the wine three times a day for 6 to 12 weeks.

Okay, we aren't really recommending this, but could snakes, or snake venom, provide unlikely relief for arthritis? Joe de Casa, a 61-year-old arthritis sufferer from Northamptonshire, certainly thinks so.

De Casa was bitten by an adder while clearing the undergrowth in his garden, and claimed that almost immediately it helped long-term arthritis pains in the hand that was bitten. He said that the months following the snake bite were the only time in the last five years that he had been pain free.

"I'd like to find another snake and invite him to bite me," he said a few months later when the snake venom had worn off and the pain returned.

The suggestion is that the snake venom acted as some sort of anti-inflammatory. Although there are no other known cases of arthritis suffers being bitten by poisonous snakes, there is anecdotal evidence of people reporting a reduction in arthritis pain following bee stings or falls in stinging nettles. The latter received some support when a small clinical study at the University of Plymouth recently demonstrated that stinging nettles can act as pain relievers.

Snakes aren't conventional treatment

also protects against heart disease.

Suggested dose: A total of 750 mg of EPA/DHA a day. Good food sources are cold-water fish such as sardines, salmon, tuna, and mackerel. Old-fashioned cod liver oil, either as a liquid, or as a tablet, is widely available, but note that it also contains high levels of vitamin A and should not be taken by pregnant women, or those planning to start a family.

GLA (Gamma Linolenic Acid)

The claim: The body converts these omega-6 fatty acids into anti-inflammatory compounds.

The proof: Studies show that GLA can reduce tenderness, and the inflammation of RA. It may reduce the need for NSAIDs such as aspirin.

Suggested dose: 1,800 mg a day. GLA is available in evening primrose oil, starflower oil, and blackcurrant seed oil. Evening primrose oil also helps relieve the symptoms associated with pre-menstrual tension.

Note: Evening Primrose oil may counteract the effects of anti-convulsant drugs.

Glucosamine Sulphate

The claim: Glucosamine sulphate can actually help the body rebuild cartilage that has been worn away, and so slow the progression of the disease. The human body produces glucosamine sulphate, but people with arthritis need more than they can produce naturally.

The proof: More than 200 volunteers took place in a three-year study in Belgium. Those taking 1,500 mg of glucosamine sulphate a day had a 20-25% improvement in symptoms, and X-rays showed that the gaps between the bones in the joints had narrowed over the three years.

Shop smart

With so many arthritis supplements on the market, it's hard to know what to buy, and what to avoid. Our 9-point check list will help:

➤ Make sure that the product label lists the amount of active ingredients it contains.

➤ Buy supplements at shops that you trust.

➤ Avoid products using words such as "miracle cure."

➤ Beware of products that claim to cure all types of arthritis.

➤ Remember: if a product sounds too good to be true, it probably is.

➤ Always talk to your doctor before starting to take any supplements for arthritis.

➤ Continue taking your current medication unless your doctor explicitly tells you not to.

➤ Bear in mind that just because something is "natural" doesn't make it effective, or safe.

➤ If you already take a supplement, tell your doctor at your next appointment.

It has also been shown to have a limited pain-killing effect. But don't forget, glucosamine comes from extract of crab, lobster, and shrimp shells, so if you are allergic to shellfish, you might not be able to take it.

Suggested dose: 1,500 mg per day.

Olive Oil

The claim: Olive oil is rich in natural antioxidants and, like fish oils, has anti-inflammatory effects.

The proof: Several studies have shown that olive oil has helped ease the symptoms of rheumatoid arthritis, although scientists still aren't sure exactly why.

Leech therapy

A study in Essen, Germany, using a small group of long-term arthritis sufferers, showed that all patients being treated with leeches found their condition improved, without any adverse side effects. It may sound like a medieval approach, but after leaving four leeches—technically known as Hirudo medicinalis—on the effected knee joints for an hour, patients reported an immediate relief from pain, and significantly less pain for up to a month afterwards.

These results backed up findings from another, wider study carried out in Russia, in which 105 arthritis sufferers (half with osteoarthritis, half with rheumatoid arthritis), were treated successfully with leeches. In this study, the patients found they had improved movement, less muscle and joint pain, and less early morning stiffness. Leech saliva contains analgesic, anaesthetic, and histamine-like compounds, and they have been used for medical purposes for 2,500 years. Scientists hope that if they can extract or recreate the substances that leeches inject into human flesh to kill pain, thin blood, and reduce inflammation then they will be able to find a new version of leech therapy without the "yuck factor."

Suggested dose: One and a half tablespoons a day, either in addition to your regular diet, or instead of other oils or fats if you are concerned about your weight. Olive oil tastes particularly good with tomato-based pasta sauces, or mixed with balsamic vinegar to make a salad dressing.

Remedies to skip

The pain and chronic nature of arthritis force some people to try anything for relief—even unproven or downright harmful remedies. When in doubt, ask your doctor for guidance. In the meantime, here are a few products that have not been proven to relieve arthritis (though some may have benefits for other conditions).

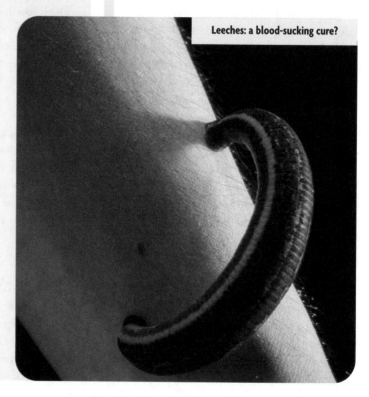

Leeches: a blood-sucking cure?

Copper bracelets: There is no scientific evidence to back up copper's anti-arthritis claims.

Shark Cartilage: There is no scientifically accepted evidence to prove this can ease arthritis, but it can cause nausea, vomiting, and fatigue.

Alfalfa: Used for years as a folk remedy for arthritis, no studies show that it is effective.

DMSO (dimethyl sulfoxide): A by-product of wood processing, DMSO is said to ease pain and improve flexibility in people with arthritis. But many versions on the market are chemically impure and potentially harmful.

Cutting out citrus fruits: Unless you have a specific food intolerance, there is no evidence that eliminating acidic citrus fruits will impact on your arthritis.

Cutting out foods from the nightshade family: There is no evidence that not eating potatoes, tomatoes, aubergines, red peppers, or chillies will alleviate arthritis, and by avoiding them you risk missing out on key vitamins and minerals.

Green-lipped mussels: Claims that it has anti-inflammatory properties have not been proven conclusively by any large-scale scientific research, although it has not been shown to be harmful in any way.

Coral calcium: The extreme longevity of people on the Japanese island of Okinawa—the average life expectancy there is more than 82—is claimed to be a result of the high levels of minerals in the water there. The theory is that the coral calcium in the drinking water, which can be bought in the West in powdered form, can boost the auto-immune system. So far, there has been no major research into the efficacy, or even the safety, of taking it as a supplement.

Cider vinegar: In contrast with the idea that you should cut out acidic citrus fruits, some people advocate taking cider vinegar to relieve arthritis symptoms. There is no scientific evidence to back this up, and remember that when it comes to acid, your stomach produces juices that are likely to be more acidic than anything you eat or drink.

Seaweed: Containing an array of minerals, especially iodine, potassium, and magnesium, Kelp, a kind of seaweed, can be taken as a food supplement, or added to bath water. But while these minerals may be beneficial to overall health, seaweed has no proven link to improving arthritis.

Selenium: Often sold in a joint formula with vitamins A, C, and E, selenium has useful anti-oxidant properties, but has been shown in scientific trial not to benefit arthritis directly.

CHAPTER 10

Eat to Beat Arthritis

Whip up these recipes. They're full of nutrients to soothe pain away

Here are some tasty recipes brimming not just with flavour but also with nutrients that may help soothe sore joints. Each dish is rich in at least one healing nutrient, such as the antioxidant vitamins A or C, and all are low in saturated fat (the type of fat that may aggravate arthritis flare-ups). We've also included a number of meals that are a fantastic source of omega-3 fatty acids, which have been shown to reduce arthritis inflammation. Whip them all up and you have a complete arthritis menu, including tasty soups and salads, light fish dishes, more substantial main meals, and two delicious desserts. We've even added a tasty fruit smoothie to blend up at any time of day.

Low-fat, tasty food to ease pain

CARROT AND ALMOND SOUP

This vitamin-rich purée served with a dollop of low-fat yoghurt cheese on top will deliver a dose of beta-carotene and plenty of antioxidant-rich vegetables. You can also serve it with a spoonful of low-fat natural yoghurt, which blends more easily with the soup when you stir it in at the table.

6 medium carrots, cut into 5 cm pieces
1 medium potato, cut into eighths
1/2 stalk celery, sliced
1 small onion, cut in half
2 shallots, cut in half
6 unblanched almonds
1/2 tsp sugar
1/2 tsp salt (optional)
1/4 tsp ground nutmeg
Pinch of ground allspice
Pinch of ground ginger
500-750 ml vegetable stock or water
4 whole cloves
2 cloves garlic, unpeeled
Ground black pepper
250 ml low-fat natural yoghurt cheese
or low-fat natural yoghurt
1 tbsp snipped chives
or spring onion stems

1 In a large non-stick saucepan, combine the carrots, potatoes, celery, onions, shallots, almonds, sugar, salt (if using), nutmeg, allspice, ginger, and 500 ml of the stock or water. Place the cloves and garlic in a mesh tea ball or wrap in a small piece of muslin and tie with kitchen string. Place in the saucepan.

2 Cover and bring almost to a boil over medium-high heat. Reduce the heat to low and simmer for 35 minutes, or until the carrots and potatoes are tender. Remove the tea ball or muslin bundle; discard the cloves. Squeeze the garlic from its skin and add the soft paste to the soup.

3 Working in batches if necessary, pour the soup into a blender or food processor. Process for several minutes, or until puréed. Return the soup to the pan. If the soup is too thick, thin with the remaining 250 ml stock or water.

4 Season to taste with the pepper. Serve topped with the yoghurt cheese or yoghurt and chives or spring onions.

Makes about 1.5 litres
Nutritional value per 250 ml: 108 kcal; 6.2 g pro; 19.7 g carb; 0.8 g total fat; 0.2 g sat fat; 1 mg chol; 2.5 g fibre 95 mg sodium

CREAM OF BROCCOLI SOUP

With a kilo of broccoli in the mix, this soup is packed with vitamin C, which will boost your immunity and help to make your blood healthier. It also offers vitamin A, as well as potassium, iron, fibre, and beta-carotene. You can make this soup into a meal by serving it over no yolk noodles, rice, or mashed potatoes.

1 kg broccoli
500 ml vegetable stock or skimmed chicken stock
1 medium onion, finely chopped
4 tbsp grated carrots
1 small clove garlic, minced
250 ml skimmed milk
250 ml low-fat liquid creamer
3 tbsp plain flour
Juice of 1 lemon
Ground black pepper
Salt (optional)
6 tbsp grated low-fat mature Cheddar cheese
1 tbsp grated mature Cheddar cheese

1 Take one bunch of the broccoli and cut the florets away from the stalks; cut the florets into slivers lengthwise and set them aside.

2 Finely chop the stalks and the remaining broccoli; place in a medium non-stick saucepan.

3 Add the stock, onions, carrots, and garlic. Cover and cook over medium heat, stirring often, for 6 to 7 minutes.

4 Add the reserved broccoli florets. Cook, stirring, for 2 to 3 minutes, or until the florets are bright green.

5 Whisk in the milk and creamer. Bring almost to a boil over medium heat.

6 Sieve the flour over the saucepan into the soup, whisking to incorporate. Cook over low heat, stirring, for 3 to 4 minutes, or until the soup is thick. Stir in the lemon juice. Season to taste with the pepper and salt (if using).

7 Serve sprinkled with both cheeses.

Makes about 2 litres
Nutritional value per 250 ml: 113 kcal; 8.7 g pro; 19 g carb; 0.9 g total fat; 0.3 g sat fat; 2 mg chol; 5 g fibre; 129 mg sodium

BARLEY-LENTIL SALAD

This hearty main-dish grain salad, or side dish, is quick and easy to make using leftover cooked barley and lentils. It's packed with vegetables and grains to boost your vitamin C reserves and fibre supplies.

8 chestnut mushrooms, sliced
2 cloves garlic, minced
125 ml skimmed chicken stock
3 tbsp balsamic vinegar
2 tsp Dijon mustard
1 tsp freshly squeezed lemon juice
250 g cooked barley
185 g cooked lentils
155 g cooked peas or thawed frozen peas
3 spring onions, sliced
8 baby carrots, sliced
1 medium tomato, diced
Ground black pepper
Salt (optional)
6 curly lettuce leaves (optional)
1 tbsp chopped fresh parsley

1 Coat a large non-stick frying pan with non-stick spray. Add the mushrooms and garlic, and mist with non-stick spray. Cover and cook over medium heat for 3 to 4 minutes, or until the mushrooms start to lose their moisture. Uncover and cook, stirring, for 1 to 2 minutes, or until the mushrooms are tender.

2 In a large bowl, combine the stock, vinegar, mustard, and lemon juice; whisk until smooth. Add the barley, lentils, peas, spring onions, carrots, tomatoes, and mushroom mixture. Toss gently to coat the salad with dressing. Season to taste with the pepper and salt (if using).

3 Line a platter with the lettuce leaves (if using). Top with the salad. Sprinkle with the parsley.

Makes 6 servings
Nutritional value per serving: 123 kcal; 6.2 g pro; 0.7 g total fat; 0.1 g sat fat; 0 mg chol; 24.5 g carb; 5.6 g fibre; 57 mg sodium

VEGETABLE LASAGNE

This scrumptious vegetable lasagne provides arthritis-healing vitamins A and C from the courgette, tomatoes, and broccoli. And because this recipe is meatless, you don't need to worry about omega-6 fatty acids, which could aggravate arthritis flare-ups.

1 teaspoon olive oil
1 courgette, chopped
450 g reduced-fat ricotta cheese
1 egg
1 tbsp dried basil
1/4 tsp salt
1/8 tsp ground black pepper
450 g spaghetti sauce
200 g lasagne
(about 9 noodles)
275 g frozen broccoli, thawed
1 can chopped tomatoes
25 g grated Parmesan cheese
25 g shredded reduced-fat mozzarella cheese

1 Preheat the oven to 170°C. Coat a medium-sized baking dish with cooking spray.

2 Warm the oil in a medium skillet over medium heat. Add the courgette, and cook for 5 minutes, or until crisp-tender. Remove from heat, and set aside.

3 In a medium bowl, mix the ricotta, egg, basil, salt, and pepper. Set aside 125 ml of the sauce.

4 Place 3 sheets of lasagne in the prepared baking dish. Evenly spoon half of the remaining spaghetti sauce over the lasagne. Top with half of the ricotta mixture, half of the broccoli, half of

the courgette, half of the tomatoes (with juice), and half of the Parmesan. Repeat layering with 3 more sheets of lasagne and the remaining ingredients. End with the remaining sheets of lasagne. Spoon the reserved sauce over the top, and sprinkle with the mozzarella.

5 Cover with foil, and bake for 25 minutes. Uncover, and bake for 20 minutes, or until hot and bubbly. Leave for 10 minutes before serving.

Makes 8 servings
Nutritional value per serving: 212 kcal;
15 g pro; 24 g carb; 6 g fat; 0 g sat fat;
43 mg chol; 4 g fibre; 881 mg sodium

GRILLED TUNA WITH HONEY-HERB SAUCE

This delicious grilled tuna steak has plenty of joint-healing omega-3 fatty acids, while the olive oil provides antioxidant protection in addition to adding great flavour.

40 g parsley, lightly packed
3 tbsp + 1 tsp olive oil
2 tbsp apple cider vinegar
2 tbsp chopped fresh dill
1½ tbsp honey
1/4 tsp salt
1/4 tsp ground black pepper
4 tuna steaks, about 2.5 cm thick and 150 g each
2 tsp capers, drained

1 Preheat the grill to medium-hot.

2 Purée the parsley, 3 tablespoons of the oil, vinegar, dill, and honey in a blender until they are a bright green, slightly thickened sauce flecked with herbs. Season with half of the salt and half of the pepper.

3 Moisten both sides of the tuna steaks with the remaining 1 teaspoon of oil, and season with the remaining salt and pepper. Grill them for a total of 5 to 6 minutes, turning once, until they are just opaque.

4 Place the tuna steaks on plates, drizzle with the sauce, and sprinkle with the capers.

Makes 4 servings
Nutritional value per serving: 311 kcal; 40 g pro; 7 g carb; 13 g fat; 2 g sat fat; 77 mg chol; 0 g fibre; 230 mg sodium

BRAISED RICE WITH MUSHROOMS

Sweet prawns and meaty mushrooms complement each other in this satisfying main course rice dish. The mushrooms act as a natural anti-inflammatory, while the drizzle of olive oil provides a shot of pain-relieving omega-3 fatty acid. This dish also makes an excellent appetiser that will serve 8.

1 large onion, chopped
185 g large flat mushrooms, sliced
4 shiitake mushroom caps, sliced
250 g short-grain white rice
300-375 ml skimmed chicken stock or water
220 g peeled prawns, cut in half lengthwise
Salt (optional)
2 spring onions, chopped
2 tbsp chopped fresh coriander
50 ml olive oil

1 Coat a large non-stick frying pan with olive oil. Add the onions and cook over medium-high heat, stirring, for 3 minutes. Add the flat mushrooms and shiitake mushrooms. Cook, stirring for 3 minutes.

2 Add the rice, mixing well. Add 125 ml of the stock or water. Cook, stirring, for 4 minutes, or until the liquid is absorbed. Add another 125 ml stock or water. Cook for 4 minutes, or until the liquid is absorbed.

3 Add the prawns and 60 ml of remaining stock or water. Cook, stirring occasionally, for 4 minutes, or until the rice is tender and the liquid is absorbed. (If the rice isn't cooked, add the remaining stock or water and continue cooking until tender.) Season to taste with the salt (if using). Stir in the spring onions and coriander.

Makes 4 servings
Nutritional value per serving: 207 kcal; 118 g prot; 38 g carb; 0.9 g fat; 0.2 g sat fat; 71 mg chol; 2.2 g fibre; 92 mg sodium

VEGETABLE STEW WITH BEEF

This stew tastes so meaty that no one would ever guess it has only 125 g of lean beef and just one gram of fat per serving, which is great because saturated fat isn't good for arthritis. Adding the carrots will provide a beta-carotene punch to your joints, and the extra apple juice provides a shot of vitamin C.

125 g lean beef topside, trimmed of all
visible fat
1 medium potato, cut into 2.5 x 1 cm strips
1 medium onion, coarsely chopped
185 g sliced carrots
125 g sliced mushrooms
2 stalks celery, cut into 2.5 cm pieces
75 g plain flour
250 ml apple juice
250 ml water
4 tbsp chopped fresh parsley
1 tsp dried rosemary, crumbled
1 tsp dried thyme
1 tsp dried basil
1 tsp dried tarragon
3 cloves garlic, thinly sliced
1 tsp ground black pepper
1 beef bouillon cube
1 vegetable bouillon cube
Salt (optional)

1 Preheat the oven to 180°C.

2 Cut the beef into 6 cm-thick slices, then into 2.5 x 1 cm strips. Place in a 3-litre baking dish. Scatter the potatoes, onions, carrots, mushrooms, and celery over the meat.

3 Place the flour in a medium bowl. Gradually whisk in the apple juice and water until smooth. Add the parsley, rosemary, thyme, basil, tarragon, garlic, and pepper. Pour over the vegetables. Add the beef bouillon cube and the vegetable bouilion cube.

4 Cover and bake for 90 minutes, or until the meat and vegetables are tender.
Season to taste with the salt (if using). Stir gently before serving.

Makes 6 servings
Nutritional value per serving: 132 kcal; 0.9 g fat; 0.3 g sat fat; 12 mg chol; 7.3 g prot; 24 g carb; 2.3 g fibre; 218 mg sodium

GINGERED VEGETABLES WITH BULGUR

This colourful dish with crisp-cooked vegetables in a savoury sauce has plenty of variety and nutrients. Every mouthful serves up a hearty pack of the antioxidants vitamin C and vitamin E, and the addition of ginger should help reduce pain for OA and RA suffers.

4 tsp of cornflour
1 tsp apricot jam
250 ml vegetable stock
1 tbsp low-sodium soy sauce
2 tsp of grated fresh ginger
2 cloves garlic, minced
125 g baby carrots, cut in quarters lengthwise
2 tbsp of chopped onions
250 g cauliflower cut into 2.5 cm pieces
125 g sliced mushrooms
1 small sweet red pepper, cut into strips
1 small yellow pepper, cut into strips
8 asparagus spears, cut in 2.5 cm lengths
45 g broccoli florets
200 g cooked bulgur
90 g cubed low-fat firm tofu
1/4 tsp toasted sesame seeds

1 In a small bowl, whisk the cornflower and jam to mix. Whisk in the stock, soya sauce, ginger, and garlic. Set aside.

2 Pour 6 mm water into a large non-stick frying pan. Add the carrots and onions. Cook over medium heat, stirring, for 3 minutes. Add the cauliflower and mushrooms; add a little more water if the pan is dry. Cover and cook for 2 minutes. Add the red peppers, yellow peppers, asparagus, and broccoli; cover and cook for 2 minutes. Pour off any excess water.

3 Add the reserved stock mixture. Cook over medium-high heat, stirring constantly, for 2 minutes, or until thickened. Stir in the bulgur. Cook for 1 to 2 minutes, or until hot.

4 Remove from the heat. Gently stir in the tofu. Sprinkle with the sesame seeds.

Makes 4 servings
Nutritional value per serving: 143 kcal; 7.2 g prot; 0.9 g fat; 0.1 g sat fat; 0 mg chol; 28.9 g carb; 6.8 g fibre; 400 mg sodium

COD BAKED IN FOIL PACKETS

As a cold water white fish, cod isn't quite as high in omega-3 fatty acids as tuna or sardines, but prepared in foil packets, it's a still low-fat meal that's quick and easy to make. Serve with a green vegetable or two, plus new potatoes, baked potatoes, carrots, or rice to add some vitamin C and beta carotene.

**4 cod fillets
(125 g each)
2 medium carrots,
julienned
1 large stalk celery,
julienned or chopped
1 onion, thinly sliced
1 tbsp capers, rinsed
and drained
1 tsp dried thyme
8 thin slices lime or
lemon
4 tbsps dry sherry or
2 tsp sherry extract
Ground black pepper
Salt (optional)**

1 Preheat the oven to 200°C.
Rinse the fish and pat dry with paper towels.

2 Place four 45 x 30 cm pieces of aluminium foil on a work surface. Tip the edges up slightly. Place one fillet in the centre of each foil piece. Sprinkle with the carrots, celery, onions, capers, and thyme.

3 Top with the lime slices or lemon slices. Sprinkle with the sherry or sherry extract, pepper, and salt (if using). Fold the edges of the foil tightly to seal, leaving some air space within each packet for steam to rise.

4 Bake for 20 minutes. Remove from the oven. Let stand for 2 to 3 minutes. Open one packet carefully, pointing it away from you to vent the hot steam. Check if it's done by inserting the tip of a sharp knife in the centre of the fillet.

5 If the fish is still translucent, close up the opened packet and return all the packets to the oven to bake for 2 to 3 minutes more. Carefully unwrap the packets. Slide the fish and vegetables onto dinner plates to serve.

Makes 4 servings
Nutritional value per serving: 101 kcal; 13.1 g pro; 6.9 g carb; 0.6 g fat; 0.1 g sat fat; 30 mg chol; 1.9 g fibre; 146 mg sodium

BLUEBERRY MOUSSE WITH RASPBERRY SAUCE

The blueberries and raspberries in this mouth-watering mousse are overflowing with healing vitamin C and antioxidants. If you'd rather not use orange liqueur, replace it with thawed frozen orange juice concentrate, which will give you additional vitamin C.

MOUSSE
1 can (325 g) evaporated milk (skimmed if possible)
50 ml cold water
2 sachets powdered gelatin
50 ml boiling water
400 g fresh or frozen blueberries (thawed)
3 tbsp orange-flavoured liqueur, such as Grand Marnier
2 tbsp lemon juice
50 g sugar

SAUCE
325 g fresh or frozen raspberries, thawed
50 g sugar
1 tbsp orange-flavoured liqueur, such as Grand Marnier
1 tsp lemon juice

1 Several hours before you plan to make the mousse, put the can of milk in the fridge to chill. Place a large metal or glass bowl, and the beaters from an electric mixer, in the freezer. (Chilling these items ensures that the milk will whip properly.)

2 Place the cold water in a small bowl, and sprinkle with the gelatin. Allow to soften for 5 minutes. Add the boiling water, and stir until the gelatin is dissolved.

3 Place the blueberries in a blender. Add the liqueur, lemon juice, and gelatin mixture. Purée. Transfer to a medium bowl, and refrigerate.

4 Remove the bowl and beaters from the freezer. Pour the chilled milk into the bowl, and beat until soft peaks form when the beaters are lifted. Slowly add the sugar, and continue beating until firm peaks form.

5 Pour the blueberry mixture over the whipped milk. Using a rubber spatula, carefully fold in the blueberry mixture until no streaks of white show. Pour into a mould, cover, and refrigerate for 4 hours.

6 To make the raspberry sauce: while the mousse is chilling, combine the raspberries, sugar, liqueur, and lemon juice in a blender. Purée. With a spatula, press through a fine strainer (to remove the seeds) into a medium bowl. Cover, and refrigerate until ready to serve.

7 Unmould the mousse onto a serving platter. Spoon into individual bowls, and top with sauce.

Makes 12 servings
Nutritional value per serving: 353 kcal; 6 g pro; 79 g carb; 2 g fat; 1 g sat fat; 6 mg chol; 9 g fibre; 333 mg sodium

FRESH FRUIT TART WITH OLIVE OIL CRUST

The French use the best and freshest ingredients so that a small portion is totally satisfying. In this case, the best fruits are also the most healing ones: apricots, kiwi fruit, and raspberries are among the top sources of vitamins A and C, both believed to help ease arthritis pain. Substituting olive oil for butter in the crust reduces the saturated fat without sacrificing flavour.

175 g plain flour
1 tbsp + 100 g sugar
1/2 tsp + 1/8 tsp salt
5 tbsp regular olive oil
1/2 tsp white vinegar
2 tbsp water
325 ml skimmed milk
1 egg
25 g cornstarch
60 g low-fat Coffee Mate or creamer
1 tsp vanilla extract
4 small apricots (or 2 small peaches), pitted and sliced into thin wedges
2 kiwi fruit, peeled and sliced into thin half-rounds
150 g fresh raspberries
Mint leaves (garnish, optional)

1 Preheat the oven to 200°C. Coat a 24 cm tart pan with cooking spray. Combine the flour, 1 tablespoon of sugar, and 1/2 teaspoon of salt in a medium bowl. Stir in the olive oil and vinegar with a fork until well combined. Add the water, stirring until the dough holds together.

2 Shape the dough into a disk, and roll between two sheets of plastic wrap into a 12^1/$_2$"- diameter circle. Freeze on a baking sheet for 15 minutes. Remove the top sheet of plastic, invert the pastry into the pan, and mould to fit. Remove the plastic, and trim the edge. Prick the dough with a fork. Bake for 16 to 18 minutes, or until golden brown.

3 To prepare the filling, whisk together the milk, egg, cornstarch, the remaining sugar, and the remaining 1/8 teaspoon of salt in a medium saucepan. Bring to a boil over medium heat, then lower the heat, whisking constantly as the mixture begins to thicken. Cook for 30 seconds, or until smooth. Gradually whisk in the creamer, and cook for 1 minute longer. Remove from the heat, and stir in the vanilla extract. Pour the filling into the warm shell, cover it with the plastic touching the surface, and chill for 2 hours or overnight.

4 Arrange the fruit in a decorative pattern on top. Garnish with mint leaves, if desired, and serve.

Makes 8 servings
Nutritional value per serving: 287 kcal; 5 g pro; 44 g carb; 10 g fat; 2 g sat fat; 28 mg chol; 2 g fibre; 185 mg sodium

MIXED FRUIT SMOOTHIE

This delicious snack or drink is a surprisingly easy way to ensure you pack in your five helpings of fruit per day. The antioxidant rich dose of vitamin C will help reduce joint pain and cartilage damage. You can make it with skimmed milk or fruit juice depending on your palate, although use sweeter apple or pineapple juices rather than any of the citrus varieties. Use this as a trial smoothie, there are an endless variety you can whip up using old fruit. Bananas act as a great base but anything like pineapple, melon or any berries work well. Try this tip: when bananas start to brown, take two, peel them, chop them into small slices and freeze them. Throw them straight from the freezer into your blender to create a mouth-watering frozen smoothie, which is perfect on a hot summer day.

1 large mango
2 ripe bananas
6-8 strawberries
10 green grapes
250 ml skimmed milk or fruit juice

1 Cut the mango into cubes or slices, add the bananas (break up into smaller pieces before putting into the blender, even if frozen), add the strawberries and grapes.

2 Pour in the skimmed milk and blend. If you used frozen ingredients, turn to the ice setting and then fully blend.

3 Serve in a cooled glass.

Serves 4
Nutritional value per serving: 95 kcal; 1.6 g pro; 20 g carb; 0.3 g fat; 0 g sat fat; 0 mg chol; 2 g fibre; 35 mg sodium

fight back against the pain

Exercise is a critical part of any anti-arthritis plan

CHAPTER 11

Arthritis-Easing Stretches

Reduce stiffness and joint pain and improve your range of motion with these moves

In just a few minutes each day, you can do something that's proven to ease arthritis stiffness and pain. All it takes are some gentle, relaxing stretches.

"The stiffness, tightness, and weakness that people with arthritis experience is often a result of not moving rather than symptoms of the disease," says chartered physiotherapist Jane Newman. Full-range movements such as stretching help relieve pain and increase mobility in joints that are inflamed by arthritis.

On the next few pages are stretches you can do throughout the day to keep your joints flexible. We've also added two specific stretches for knee and wrist pain. (If you have inflammatory rheumatoid arthritis, check with your GP or physiotherapist before beginning a stretching programme.)

Stretch gently to combat pain

A Day of Soothing Stretches

7AM: REDUCE STIFFNESS AND RELIEVE BACK PAIN

[1] Kneel on your hands and knees with your head, neck, and back in alignment. Keeping your shoulders relaxed, lower your chin towards your chest, pull in your stomach, and round your back, like a cat arching. (Where you'll feel it: throughout your back and shoulders.) Hold, then slowly return to the starting position. [2] Next, arch your back, creating an inward curve with your bottom lifted towards the ceiling and your head looking up just slightly. (Where you'll feel it: throughout your back and abdominals.) Hold, then repeat the sequence.

10AM: RELIEVE MUSCLE TENSION

Sit on the edge of a chair with your pelvis tilted slightly forward and your legs spread as wide as comfortable. Slide your chin back so that your ears align over your shoulders. Lift your chest, and squeeze your shoulder blades together and down, away from your ears. Reach both arms wide and slightly behind you. Your palms should be facing forward, fingers spread. Don't arch your lower back. (Where you'll feel it: chest, shoulders, and upper back.) Hold, then repeat.

FRONT VIEW

1PM: REDUCE HIP PAIN

Stand with your feet a few inches apart, then move one leg about 1 to 2 feet forward. Bend your knees, making sure your front knee is directly over the ankle. Your back heel will come off the floor. Keep your posture upright as you tuck in your abdomen and bottom and tilt your pelvis. Hold. (Where you'll feel it: front of hips.)

Stretch Away Knee and Wrist Pain

The knees and wrists are joints often affected by arthritis. Here are stretches to help soothe the pain and increase the range of motion.

EASE KNEE PAIN

While sitting with your knees bent, gently extend one foot at a time forwards and backwards. Do this 5 to 10 times with each leg. (This stretch is great if you've been sitting for a long time.)

REDUCE WRIST PAIN

While seated with your forearms resting in front of you on a small desk or table, clasp your hands and intertwine your fingers. Bend both wrists to the right, hold for about 5 seconds, then bend your wrists to the left and hold, and repeat several times. Next, move your arms forward so that your hands are off the table edge. Moving just your wrists, lift your hands towards the ceiling, and hold for about 5 seconds, repeating several times. Then lower toward the floor, and hold.

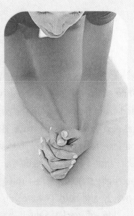

10 commandments of stretching

➤ Follow a programme that is specific to your activities and needs.

➤ Stretch regularly, at least three times a week.

➤ Warm up before stretching.

➤ Stretch only until you feel tension in the muscle, not pain in the joint.

➤ Hold each stretch for 15 to 60 seconds.

➤ Do each stretch 2 to 4 times.

➤ Stay relaxed.

➤ Breathe throughout the stretch.

➤ Progress in a slow, controlled manner.

➤ Don't bounce.

3PM: EASE NECK PAIN

While sitting in a chair, hook your left hand, palm facing you, on the back of the seat next to your left buttock. Hold on as you lean forwards. Keep your shoulders back, and drop your right ear towards your right shoulder. Then roll your chin forwards, and hold. (Where you'll feel it: left side of neck.) Switch hands, and repeat on the other side.

REAR VIEW

6PM: LOOSEN UP YOUR TORSO

[1] Stand up straight with your feet shoulder-width apart, hips facing forward, and abs tight. Gently twist your trunk to the right, and hold. (Where you'll feel it: abs, sides, and back.) Return to the starting position, and repeat to the left. [2] Next, gently lean to the right as you reach your left arm up towards the ceiling, curve it slightly overhead, palm down. Keep your shoulders down and relaxed. Hold, then repeat to the left side. (Where you'll feel it: sides of your torso.)

8PM: IMPROVE POSTURE AND MUSCLE TONE

[1] Stand with your feet shoulder-width apart and your abs tight. Keeping your back straight, bend at the hips and knees, reaching your hands through your legs, if comfortable. Hold. Caution: don't do this if you have back pain. (Where you'll feel it: bottom and thighs.)

[2] Next, use your hips to straighten up, reaching your arms overhead and slightly behind you. Hold. Don't arch your back. (Where you'll feel it: chest, upper back, shoulders, and abs.) Repeat the entire sequence.

10PM: REDUCE SHOULDER PAIN AND RELAX FOR SLEEP

Lie on the floor on your right side with your right arm bent underneath your head. Bend both legs so you're comfortable. Imagine that you're lying on a big clock. Extend your left arm in front of you on the floor as if it's a clock hand pointing to 9 o'clock. Slowly rotate your arm towards 12 o'clock. As you hit 1 o'clock, you'll start to roll back, but keep your hips and legs where they are. Keeping your arm on the floor, rotate it through all the numbers on the clock (your palm will flip up momentarily behind you), over your hips, and back to the starting position. (Where you'll feel it: shoulders and upper back, then chest and middle back, and finally hips and lower back.)

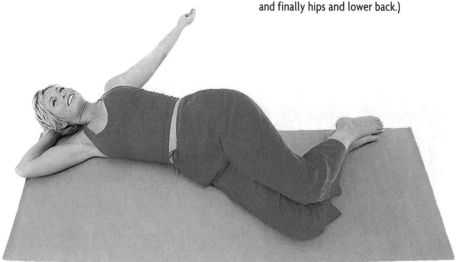

CHAPTER 12

The Simple Way to Walk Off Weight and Ease Arthritis

This little device will motivate you to lose pounds—no tough workout required!

What magical gadget are we talking about? It's the simple pedometer, traditionally used by race walkers to track their mileage. But this unimpressive-looking device may be one of the most powerful motivators you've ever encountered, short of a traditional Army Drill Sergeant.

Track your progress with a pedometer

Studies now show that sedentary people who wear pedometers and have a daily goal become more active all day and see improvements in fitness and body fat comparable to people doing more structured exercise.

If you're one of those people who believe that only vigorous exercise—such as jogging 2 miles—counts toward fitness, you'd better think again, says Dr Ross Andersen from Johns Hopkins School of Medicine in Baltimore, USA. The pedometer research that Dr Andersen and others have done shows that just increasing your everyday activities—walking the dog or getting out more often—makes a big difference.

The truth is that something as simple as walking is often overlooked as a way of keeping fit and flexible. But it's the simplicity that makes it such a great exercise for many people. We all know how to do it, it's inexpensive and you can walk anywhere, at any time and at any level you prefer on a particular day.

And there are even more benefits if you have arthritis: not only will this increase in physical activity enable you to drop pounds and take weight off aching joints, but it will also help alleviate your arthritis pain by aiding in the stabilization of your joints.

It works as a preventative tool too. As a weight-bearing exercise (one that puts full weight on your bones), walking helps strengthen bones, reducing the long term risk of osteoporosis (thinning of the bones). This is especially important if you are taking glucocorticoids for arthritis, which can weaken bones.

Walking can also reap psychological benefits. Regular exercise helps you to sleep better, controls your weight, and lifts your spirits. It can play an important part in combating the depression, fatigue, and stress that accompany your arthritis.

So we decided to give it a try. We put a group of overweight people on a pedometer-based walking programme. Based on the number of steps they normally took, we

Walking with friends is the way to go

divided them into two groups. Those who were inactive had a goal of 10,000 steps, while those who were more active had a goal of 18,000 steps. After just 8 weeks, they saw improvements in weight, body fat, cholesterol, and fitness levels.

Special Benefits for Arthritis Sufferers

Not only is walking terrific for relieving painful, stiff joints and boosting stamina, but your sense of well-being will also increase as you gain freedom of movement, says arthritis

LESS EFFORT, GREATER RESULTS

Annette Burke, 39

EXECUTIVE ASSISTANT

◆ Increased activity by 9,950 steps a day
◆ Dropped 5 lb
◆ Lowered cholesterol by 24 points
◆ Cut 1-mile walk time by more than 3 minutes

After cycling and spinning on and off for 4 years, Annette was surprised that a walking programme could deliver results. "It was so easy. I'd just slip the pedometer on every morning."

Tips:

◆ Parking her car farther away.
◆ Taking the longest route to other offices.
◆ Using the stairs instead of the lift.
◆ Doing periodic "step checks" helped Annette stay on target, so she wasn't left with a huge amount of walking to do after work.

Results:

By incorporating more walking throughout the day, Annette found a new stress reducer that gave her a real energy boost during the afternoon slump.

BEFORE

expert Shannon Mescher. Here are some things Mescher recommends you do as part of a walking programme. Use these tips alongside our pedometer plan.

➤ Wear shoes designed for aerobic activity, such as walking or running shoes.

➤ Make sure your shoes fit correctly, ideally you should have a thumb nail's worth of space between the end of your toes and the end of the shoes. Also make sure the shoes fit firmly around the heel to stabilize your feet where you're walking.

➤ Walk regularly on a flat surface, three to five times a week, for 20 to 30 minutes—all at once or in several shorter sessions.

➤ Take the time to warm up and cool down before and after you've walked.

➤ Walk at your own pace, everyone has a

Finding a Pedometer

There is a wide range of pedometers available either at outdoor sports shops or specialist walking or running stores. The model on page 106 is the Silva Pedometer Plus (£14.95; www.gear-zone.co.uk or www.adventureshop.co.uk). It's a lightweight compact model with an extra large display that counts the number of steps taken, shows distance and the number of calories consumed.

walking speed that suits them best, so find one that's comfortable for you. Remember that your comfortable pace may vary from day to day.

➤ Time your walking sessions for when you feel at your best. Perhaps you are at your most energetic first thing in the morning, or it may be that you feel less stiff in the afternoon.

➤ Log your walks. You'll stay motivated by your progress.

➤ Get help. Walking poles can relieve lower-body stress. Velcro closure trainers mean no painful lacing. You can find both at sports shops or outdoors shops nationwide.

CASE STUDY
"I Walked Away from Arthritis Pain!"

When she was diagnosed with rheumatoid arthritis and ankylosing spondylitis 10 years ago, Hilary Wilson, 51, never dreamed there'd be a marathon in her future. But last October, she walked 26.2 miles in Dublin. "Now I know I can take on any challenge," she says. The Arthritis Research Campaign organizes walks all over the UK. Call them on 0870 850 500, or go to www.arc.org.uk to find out more.

How the Pedometer Helps You Succeed

It's inexpensive, low-tech, and doesn't require any expertise. You just snap it on and look at it every

---

TAKE CONTROL

Mix it up and find a friend

It's the simplicity of walking that makes it so appealing to so many people. But that can sometimes make it difficult to stay motivated, particularly if walking is your primary means of exercise. Here are a couple of quick ideas to make your walking time more interesting.

Switch location

If you always walk in the same routes in the same area, walking will be tedious. Treat your walks as an adventure, a means of exploring new areas or an excuse to visit different places. Plan your holidays around good places to walk.

Phone a friend

It's always easier to let yourself down than someone else. There is no better way to ensure you stick with your walking routine than recruiting a friend to join you. It's a lot more fun to do it this way too; the walk becomes less a means of taking exercise and more of a social occasion. You don't have to limit yourself to one friend either.

now and then. The greatest power of the pedometer, though, is its ability to motivate. Lots of people will give you messages—for example, they might suggest simple measures such as parking further away or taking the stairs instead of the lift—but when you're wearing a pedometer, you can see the difference. It also cues you to be more active. When you see or feel the pedometer on your waistband, you're reminded to get moving, especially if you have a long way to hit your goal.

Even Exercisers Can Benefit

If you already exercise but aren't seeing the results that you would like, a pedometer may be the answer. Because of labour-saving devices, our daily activity has almost diminished to nil. So your regular exercise sessions may not be enough to counteract what you're not burning. By using a pedometer, you'll be reminded to be more active during the day.

A LITTLE HELP FROM MY FRIENDS
Linda Fry, 43
CUSTOMER SERVICE SPECIALIST

- Increased activity by 5,496 steps a day
- Dropped 7 lb
- Lost 41/4 inches off waist, hips, and thighs
- Lowered cholesterol by 32 points

After realizing that her sedentary office job only afforded her a maximum of 3,500 steps during the workday, Linda had to come up with some creative ideas to reach her daily goal of 10,000 steps.

BEFORE

Tips:
- Walking, instead of driving, to local destinations (including work) was a good start.
- Starting her own walking club as a fun way to incorporate more steps. Each day, she would ask someone new to walk with her. The support and enthusiasm of her close friends were perfect motivators.

Results:
Not only was Linda losing pounds and inches, but she also had more energy and could climb stairs without huffing and puffing. And by staying off the couch, she's realized that she can keep off the weight while still eating the same amount of food.

You Can Do It Too

Just follow our step-by-step plan to boost your own weight loss and fitness efforts.

Step 1: Determine how much activity you're currently getting. To do that, wear a pedometer for at least 3 days—from the time you get out of bed until you go to sleep at night. Do what you normally do. If you don't usually walk at lunch, don't start now. Try to measure at least 1 weekend day, since activity levels vary from weekdays.

Step 2: Calculate your baseline by averaging your step counts for the 3 days.

Step 3: Go to the chart below, and circle the range in column A that includes your baseline number.

Step 4: Determine your ultimate goal by adding 7,500 steps to your baseline.

Step 5: Go down column B, and circle the number closest to your ultimate goal.

Step 6: Go back to the number you circled in column A, and work your way across the row.

Column B is your initial goal, column C tells you how many more steps you need to take to reach this goal, and column D shows you about how long it will take. (If you're on the lower end of the range in column A, you will be on the higher end of the range in column D, and vice versa.) If you need more time, take it.

Step 7: Once you have achieved your initial goal, move on to the next row. Continue until you reach the number circled in column B (your ultimate goal).

Step 8: Maintain your ultimate goal for at least 8 weeks. If you're no longer getting results from this level of activity, you could increase your daily steps. If you don't have time for more walking, focus instead on increasing your intensity by going faster or including more hills.

Goal: Increase the number of steps you usually take by 7,500—the average increase that our participants achieved.

A	B	C	D
If your baseline is...	Your goal is... (initial and ultimate goals)	How to reach your goal (increase by)	Time needed to reach goal
Less than 2,500 steps	5,000	250 steps per day	10–20 days
2,501–5,000 steps	7,500	300 steps per day	8–16 days
5,001–7,500 steps	10,000	400 steps per day	6–12 days
7,501–10,000 steps	12,500	500 steps per day	5–10 days
10,001–12,500 steps	15,000	500 steps per day	5–10 days
12,501–15,000 steps	17,500	750 steps per day	3–6 days
15,001–17,500 steps	20,000	750 steps per day	3–6 days

Example: If your baseline is 5,025, your ultimate goal would be 12,525. To reach it, first aim for a total of 10,000 steps. To do that, walk an extra 400 steps a day for about 12 days. Your next goal would be 12,500 steps—your ultimate goal—so you'd add 500 steps a day for 5 days.

CHAPTER 13

Soothe Sore Joints With a Water Walking Workout

Let the natural buoyancy of water help you exercise in comfort

For people with arthritis, water can be your biggest ally when it comes to exercise. Why? If you have arthritis, warm-water exercise can encourage your stiff joints to become more flexible, while relaxing your tight muscles. The buoyancy of the water supports your joints. Yet water also provides resistance. Pushing against it as you move through it helps build up strength. "And water walking is a wonderful aerobic exercise," says physiotherapist Kathleen Ferrell.

Water exercise can usually be continued during flare-ups because the warmth and buoyancy help decrease pain and stiffness and make movement much easier.

Reap the benefits of warm-water exercises

But you'll need some guidance from your doctor or physiotherapist on how hard to push yourself when you are having a flare-up. Ferrell has devised a water-walking workout especially for *Outsmart Arthritis* readers.

Your Joint Protection Programme

The basic components of any fitness programme are cardiovascular training (which works the heart and lungs), strength training, and flexibility exercises. The latter is particularly important to help arthritis sufferers ease their pain and stay active.

Our water-walking workout addresses all three fitness components with a combination of low-impact walking and range-of-motion exercises. And since arthritis can affect any joint, this is a total-body programme, so it's sure to include your problem area as well as improve full-body fitness.

It's important to complement your water workouts with regular strength training. Work with your doctor or arthritis specialist to devise a strength plan that works for you.

TAKE CONTROL

Stay Vertical

When you start an aqua-walking or aqua-running session, work on your posture, by trying to remain upright. Using a flotation device will help, but try to keep your ears, hips and shoulders in line. Tighten your stomach muscles to prevent you from slouching forward.

Technique. Standing in water that's between hip- and waist-deep, start walking, swinging your arms in time with your legs. Start slowly, then pick up speed. Work up to a comfortable, brisk pace.

Duration and intensity. Start with 5 minutes of water walking, then gradually increase the time until you feel it could be rated as moderate, which America's Arthritis Foundation describes as anywhere from "still light, but starting to work" to "still comfortable, but harder" to "getting to be somewhat hard."

Why Water Exercise?

➤ Immersing in water raises your body temperature, causing your blood vessels to dilate, and increasing circulation.

➤ The warmth and buoyancy of the water in swimming pools makes it an ideal environment for relieving arthritis pain and stiffness.

➤ Water supports joints in a weight-free environment to encourage free movement, and it may also act as resistance to help build muscle strength.

➤ It's a gentle way to exercise joints and muscles.

➤ Add to the therapy by relaxing in a spa, using water as a massage tool. Jet nozzles release warm water and air, massaging your body and helping you to relax tight muscles.

YOUR WATER WARM-UP

To avoid pain and injury, a warm-up is essential for all exercisers—but especially for people with arthritis. Start with the following set of full-body, range-of-motion exercises that will increase your flexibility.

Walk into the water to chest height. The body part you're exercising should be underwater. You'll need to go into deeper water or crouch down to get your shoulders underwater when doing the first two exercises. Do all of these moves slowly. Never stretch to the point of pain or discomfort.

Do at least three repetitions of each of these moves. Depending on your individual needs and condition, you

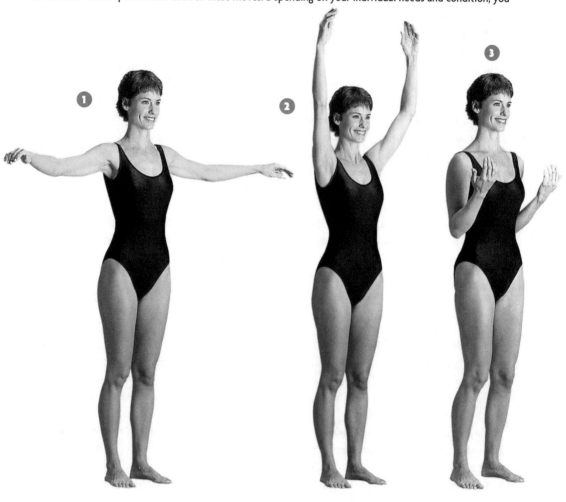

can do as many as 10 of any move to help loosen stiff joints. Repeat the entire set of exercises to cool down after your water-walking programme.

1. Swing your arms out to the sides.
2. Lift your arms over your head.
3/4. Bend and straighten your elbows.
5/6. Bend and straighten your wrists.
7. With each hand held in a loose fist, bend and straighten your fingers.

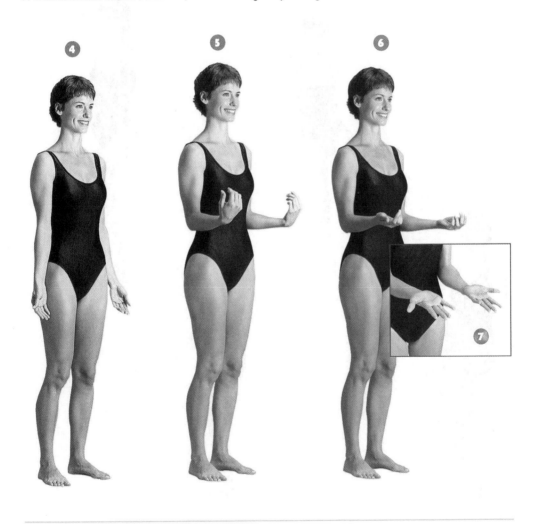

THE PROGRAMME

After completing your water warm-up, you're ready to exercise. Do the following routine after trying the water walking described on page 113. Try to do this session three to five times per week.

1. Take high steps, lifting your raised knee towards your chest. If your knees are sore, and this is uncomfortable, bend them behind you.

2. Standing on one leg, swing the other leg out to the side; then switch sides.

3. Flex and extend each ankle (up, then down).

4. Extend each ankle; move each ankle in a circle.

Stepping up the pace

If you are looking for a more vigorous form of exercise in the water, you can try aqua jogging or aqua running, which was developed in the 1980s to help competitive athletes who were suffering from injuries. The principles are much the same as for aqua walking: by using the water to take the weight off your body and your joints, you can do exercises in the water that might otherwise be difficult and painful on dry land. The significant difference here is that you should do the exercise in deeper water without your feet touching the bottom of the pool, and since you are running rather than walking, it's almost a second-stage programme to build up to. Since you are using deeper water, you should think about doing it with a simple buoyancy aid, such as an Aquajogger (£30 from **www.aquajogger.co.uk**) that straps around your waist in order to keep you afloat, and helps you maintain an upright body position. Here are a few tips to help you with the transition from walking to running.

➤ Begin a session with the same easy warm-up that you use for walking.

➤ The ideal body position for running (as with walking) is the same as it is on land, upright with a slight lean forward. But don't lean too far forward, which is the natural tendency.

➤ Your arm swing should be as natural as it would be if you were running outside.

➤ You are aiming to build-up to a continuous aerobic session of 20 minutes.

➤ Start by running for one minute and walking for one, gradually increasing the length of the running segments while maintaining the short walking periods.

➤ Maintain a level of exertion that allows you to keep your breathing even and under control. Don't hold your breath as you would if swimming.

➤ The water line, even with a buoyancy aid, should be at shoulder level.

➤ Don't bob. Try to maintain a steady cadence, and keep your head above water.

➤ Wear goggles. If your face is constantly in the water, the pool chemicals can irritate your eyes, especially early in the morning.

Aqua jogging: ultra-low-impact running

CHAPTER 14

Get Fit, Firm and Pain Free

Cutting-edge research shows that strength training protects joints and reduces pain

For people with arthritis, the adage, "exercise is the best medicine" could not be more true. But *Outsmart Arthritis* wants to slightly edit that phrase to say, "strength training is the best medicine."

In a study at Tufts University in Boston, USA, researchers took 46 people with arthritis (all of whom reported significant amounts of pain) and divided them into a strength-training group and a non-strength-training group. After 4 months, the exercise group reported a 43% decrease in pain compared with only 12% of the non-exercisers. The strength training group also reported a 44% increase in physical improvement.

Researchers found that strength training just three times a week improves physical function and decreases pain.

Why is strength training so effective? The stronger the muscles around your joints, the greater the pressure they take off those joints, which then helps to protect them from further damage.

Then you have the other fabulous benefits of strength training that can only help those with arthritis: you become more self-sufficient, your emotional outlook improves, and you feel better in general.

Here is a basic and easy strength-training programme that targets the muscles that protect your joints. In just a few weeks, you'll feel better—and look great too! (As with all exercise programmes, check with your GP or physiotherapist before starting the strength-training programme.)

Get into the swing of strength training

Build strength, reduce knee pain

If you're suffering from osteoarthritis of the knee, then you'll want to act on research from the Medical College of Georgia in the USA. In the study, 135 participants were randomly placed into groups that either took part in a 16-week strength-training programme or did no exercise at all. And after three sessions of 20 to 30 minutes of exercise a week, the strength-trainers showed a 20 per cent increase in physical functioning and about a 50 per cent decrease in pain.

What to Do

◆ Aim for 1 set of 12 repetitions three times a week (except for the Chest Lift). Over time, work up to 2 sets of 12 repetitions each.

◆ When required, use 1-, 2-, 3-, or 5-lb dumbbell weights—or none at all if you're just starting—depending on what you can handle. Increase the dumbbell weight as you get stronger.

STEP UP
(Strengthens front and back of thighs as well as hips)

Stand facing an aerobic step (or a regular stair), with hands at your sides. Place your left foot completely on the step. Pull up and forward with your left leg to bring your right foot up to the step. Step back off with the right foot. The left foot remains on the step until you have completed all the repetitions for that leg. Then switch legs and repeat.

SQUAT

(Strengthens inner, front, and back of thighs)

Stand with your back to a chair and your feet about shoulder-width apart. Keeping your back straight, bend at the knees and hips as though you are sitting down. Don't let your knees move forward beyond your toes. Stop just shy of touching the chair, then stand back up again. (Start without dumbbells. As you progress, hold a dumbbell in each hand.)

CHEST PRESS

(Strengthens chest and front of shoulders)

Lying on the floor (or a bench), hold the dumbbells end to end just above chest height; your elbows should be pointing out. Press the dumbbells straight up, extending your arms. Hold, then lower.

CALF RAISE
(Strengthens calf muscles and improves ankle mobility)

Stand with your feet about hip-width apart. If you need balance support, hold on to a chair. Slowly rise up onto your toes while keeping your torso and legs straight. Hold, then lower.
(Start without dumbbells. As you progress, hold a dumbbell in each hand. Do the same for the Step Up.)

CHEST LIFT
(Strengthens back and buttock muscles)

Lie face down on the floor with your hands under your chin. Lift your head, chest, and arms about 5 to 6 inches off the floor. Hold for 3 to 5 seconds, then lower. Repeat 5 times.
(If too difficult, place your hands at your sides.)

Get Stronger to Reduce Knee and Hip Pain

FOR YOUR KNEES

This exercise strengthens the quadriceps, which are the muscles in the front of the thighs that support your knees.

Sit in a chair with your feet flat on the floor. Loop an exercise band around your left ankle, or use a light ankle weight. Rest your palms on the sides of the chair for support. Slowly lift your left foot until your leg is straight.

Hold for a second or two, then slowly lower. Continue until your leg feels tired, then repeat with your right leg.

FOR YOUR HIPS

This exercise, which was recommended by Dr Art Brownstein, author of *Healing Back Pain Naturally* (Harbor Press, 1999), stretches and strengthens the muscles of the hips.

Lying on your back, bend both knees together, and bring them towards your chest. Then slowly move them in an ever-widening circle, keeping your lower spine on the floor. After you do 5 to 10 circles, switch direction. Then slowly come back to your original position.

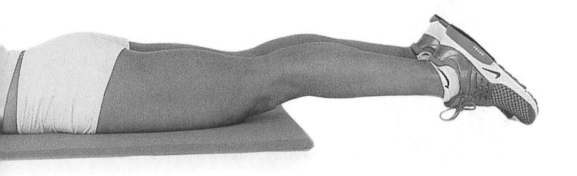

CHAPTER 15

Expand Your Exercise Horizons, Liberate Your Life

Even with arthritis your exercise options are broader than you think

To the initiated, exercise and arthritis seem unlikely bedfellows. After all, if you have sore joints and stiff limbs, you're not going to be able to participate or enjoy physical activity, are you? Wrong. Arthritis definitely shouldn't stop you from taking part in sport. In fact, having arthritis is an excellent reason to get active. By stretching and strengthening muscles, putting joints through a wide range of motion, and burning calories to help you lose weight, exercise and sport are proven paths to pain relief. Over the next 6 pages you'll find an activity to suit you and your arthritis.

Age is no excuse for inactivity

A Chinese approach to pain relief

Tai Chi

Tai chi, a Chinese exercise that strengthens muscles, improves balance and flexibility, and promotes relaxation, may have a huge side benefit—relief of chronic joint pain.

In a US study of people suffering from chronic arthritis pain, researchers found that those who attended weekly hour-long tai chi classes had significantly less pain than those not taking the class. "Tai chi increases circulation, which may improve joint function," says researcher Patricia Alder, from Cape Western University. "It also stabilizes the joint structure and strengthens the soft tissue that supports the joint, which may help reduce pain."

And another study found that after 12 weeks of trying a specially designed tai-chi programme, women with osteoarthritis suffered less pain, were less stiff, and found it easier to perform everyday tasks.

In fact, one of the researchers behind this study, Australian doctor and tai chi instructor Paul Lam, has developed a tai chi programme especially for arthritis patients. It uses slow, continuous, and gentle movements that help painlessly strengthen muscles and joints, boost flexibility, and improve balance.

There are now a large number of instructors in the UK teaching Lam's Tai Chi for Arthritis all over the country. Visit **www.arthritis.com** to find an instructor near you, or purchase the Tai Chi for Arthritis video from **www.amazon.co.uk**. Alternatively, simply look for a tai chi class at your local gym.

Swimming

For a whole body workout, it's hard to beat swimming. And the good news is that the pool is the perfect place for people with arthritis to exercise.

Swimming stretches and strengthens

Pull out your driver

It doesn't matter whether you've played golf for years or you are new to the fairways, arthritis doesn't have to stop you playing golf. In fact, golf can help your arthritis – it can enhance the strength and mobility of your upper body, and stretch out joints and muscles. And don't forget the benefits you will get from doing all that walking.

virtually every muscle in your body and provides a gentle cardiovascular workout at the same time. The best thing about it, though, is that it's impact free. In the pool, water supports your bodyweight, so your joints won't be jarred or strained as you put them through a wide range of motion.

Of course, it's important that you find a stroke that's comfortable for you. Many arthritis sufferers find that breast stroke—one of the gentlest swimming strokes—is actually one of the most painful. That's because it can put too much strain on your knees and hips. And if you keep your head out of the water as you swim, be careful—this can put extra pressure on your neck.

Before you use a pool, check a couple of things. Firstly, ensure that you'll be able to get in out of the pool easily and safely. Some people with arthritis find it difficult to use ladders to get out of the water, so look for a pool with steps at the shallow end. You also need to check the pool's temperature: The warmer the better. Warm water soothes and relaxes muscles and joints. Often, the children's pool is heated to a warmer temperature than the main baths. Finally, check for deep water. If you can get in and out easily, the

deeper the water, the more it'll support your joints and muscles.

Even if you can't swim, the pool is an excellent place to exercise. The bouyancy provided by water can make exercises that are difficult on land far easier, and it also provides natural resistance to build strength. Most local swimming pools offer aqua aerobics classes, and many cater for people with restricted mobility. Start with an easy class, and make the instructor aware of your condition.

Or ask at your hospital about hydrotherapy courses. Held under the supervision of a physiotherapist, these take place in a pool heated to a temperature similar to a warm bath. You'll need a referral from your GP to attend a class, but even if there isn't a hydrotherapy facility close by, ask your physio-therapist for exercises that you can adapt for your local pool.

Cycling

Don't let arthritis stop you from getting on your bike. In fact, cycling is yet another sport that, as well as boosting your stamina, strength, and balance, can help relieve pain and swelling.

A review of studies of people with fibromyalgia syndrome by the Cochrane Musculoskeletal Group found that people with FMS who did aerobic exercises such as cycling for 6 to 20 weeks appeared to improve their pain thresholds, experience less pain and boost their overall sense of well-being.

A word of caution before you get into the saddle, though. Cycling isn't ideal for all people with arthritis—especially those with knee problems. Check with your GP or physiotherapist first, and use some common sense.

Once you've got the all-clear, there are a few things you can do to get the most from your bike rides. The most important consideration, whether you're cycling outside or indoors, is the fit of your bike. Too small or too big, and rather than helping, your bike may exacerbate your pain levels. You should be able to straighten your leg when the ball of your foot is resting on the pedal at its lowest position and your arms should be bent slightly at the elbows when you're gripping the handlebars. If you're planning on buying a new bike, ask for fitting advice in a good bike shop.

If you have arthritis in your hands, a good pair of cycling gloves can actually relieve pressure on your painful joints. And look for a bike with a "grip shift" that lets you use your whole hand to change gear rather than just your thumbs. Some exercise bikes have handlebars that allow you to lean forward and put your weight on your forearms—perfect for people suffering from sore wrists and elbows.

Once you're pedalling, don't strain. Warm up for at least 15 minutes in a very low gear to get the blood flowing and your joints loose. And once you're riding properly, resist the temptation to change up through the gears to work hard. Instead, "spin" in a low gear that lets you pedal quickly and with little resistance.

Get on your bike to relieve pain

Yoga

If you assume that yoga is simply about twisting your body into impossible poses, then you'll also assume that it's not for people with arthritis. You're wrong on both counts.

Of course, there are some dynamic forms of this ancient exercise that only the strongest and most supple can do, but yoga can also be a gentle way to stretch muscles, increase flexibility, and feel great. Better still, it's also been shown to help arthritis sufferers.

A study by researchers at the University of Pennsylvania

in the USA found that by taking part in an eight-week yoga programme, people with osteoarthritis of the hands experienced significantly less pain and tenderness, and improved range of motion. Another study, published in the journal *Rheumatic Disease Clinics of North America* also found that yoga could help ease pain associated with osteoarthritis.

If you're interested in trying yoga, here are a few pointers to help you on the way.

Book a class: It can be tempting to try and learn yoga from a book or video, especially if you're worried about your ability. However, it's much easier and safer to learn yoga from an experienced instructor who'll ensure that you are performing the moves correctly.

Look for qualifications: The British Wheel of Yoga is the governing body for yoga in the UK, and trains people to provide a recognized qualification for yoga teachers. You can find BWY fully qualified teachers in your area at **www.bwy.org.uk** or call **01529 306851**. Ask if they are familiar with arthritis and the therapeutic use of yoga.

Go gently: Some of the yoga classes taught can be pretty tough and aren't suitable for people with arthritis. It's sensible to look for gentle forms of yoga, such as hatha or sivanada, that use slow, easy moves.

Check with your doctor: Find out if there are any moves you need to avoid, and then let your instructor know!

Pilates

During the first world war, a nurse called Joseph Pilates developed a new method of body conditioning to help rehabilitate wounded soldiers. After the war, the former gymnast started using his exercise method to help injured dancers. More than 80 years later, Pilates is hugely popular. And it is perfect for people with arthritis.

Pilates involves a series of gentle, controlled movements that strengthen your deep abdominal muscles to improve your balance and coordination, while stretching and strengthening other muscles. It's a wonderful, low-impact exercise that puts little strain on your joints.

The stretching done during a Pilates workout—either on mats or special machines—is especially good for arthritis sufferers, as they increase flexibility, loosen up tight joints and muscles and, for many people, help reduce pain and fatigue. Pilates also helps gently improve posture—and good posture can help ease arthritis aches.

Unlike yoga, there's no recognized national governing body for Pilates, so look for an instructor who has spent several years training and who can show you an up-to-date insurance certificate. And tell them about your condition so that they can provide suitable exercises.

Although there is no nationally recognized governing body for Pilates, good instructors will have spent several years training, and will also update their skills annually to retain their insurance certificates. (You can find trained instructors at **www.bodycontrol.co.uk**, or call **020 7379 3734**). Sit in on a class before you sign up, and look for a small group of between 10-15 participants so that the instructor can spend time one-to-one with you. Alternatively, try the gentle beginners' Pilates moves found in books such as Denise Austin's *Pilates for Everybody*. (Rodale Books, £12.99)

Jogging strengthens bones, muscles and tendons

Running

It's pretty much guaranteed that at some time in the past you've heard somebody say: "Don't run, it'll play havoc with your joints when you're older." For years, people assumed that pounding the pavements was a sure-fire way to give yourself arthritis of the knees and ankles when you were older. Thankfully for runners, there's now plenty of evidence that shows the complete opposite is true, and that lacing up your trainers is actually good for your joints.

One of the most recent long-term studies, carried out at Stanford University in the USA, followed 961 people for several years. In the study, 538 were runners, while the other 423 never did any exercise. At the end of the study, 20% of the non-exercisers experienced pain and disability due to osteoporosis compared with just 5% of the runners. The runners also had greater bone density and lost less bone mineral than the couch potatoes.

But what if you already suffer from arthritis—is running any use then? Yes, it is. Not only does gentle jogging help strengthen your bones, but it also makes the muscles and tendons that support your joints stronger. And as it's a weight-bearing exercise, it encourages the production of synovial fluid—our joints' natural lubricant.

Of course, consult your doctor before you start running, as it won't be suitable for everybody with arthritis. But if you can start, here are a few tips to get you running.

Choose a good shoe: Visit a specialist running retailer so that you get the best possible advice on footwear. Every runner needs a shoe that's perfectly matched to the way they run. The right shoe will provide you with enough support and cushioning to make running as comfortable as possible.

Start slowly: The best way to begin a running programme is to mix jogging and walking. Start by walking for one minute, then jogging for one minute, then walking for one minute, and so on. Do this for 10 to 30 minutes, gradually increasing the length of your jogs and cutting back the walking.

Look for soft ground: Even if a runner has no history of arthritis, they should avoid jogging on hard surfaces such as concrete and Tarmac. Forest trails and grass paths in parks are the best places to run. Even treadmills in gyms are softer than pavements!

Stretch yourself: After every run gently stretch the muscles in your legs. Pay particular attention to your quadriceps, hamstrings, and calves.

For beginners' running programmes, stretching tips, and shoe information visit **www.runnersworld.co.uk.**

CHAPTER 16

Psychology of Arthritis

Your mind and your faith can be powerful weapons in the battle against pain

When you are diagnosed with arthritis of any type, a future of chronic pain can be a terrifying thought. Family and friends will be able to see any physical limitations that your arthritis causes, and they will be able to work with you to overcome them, but your pain can leave you isolated. It hurts, and it is going to go on hurting. And while pain-killing drugs play a vital role in arthritis treatment, the emotional impact of being in pain every day can have a devastating effect on not only the patient, but those around them too. That's why it is essential to learn to manage your pain, and develop strategies to minimize its impact on your life.

Think your way pain-free

Often the prospect of future suffering can be as damaging as the actual current pain itself. Dr Amanda Williams, Consultant Clinical Psychologist at St Thomas's Hospital in London, says that these fears are not surprising, given that many people's knowledge of arthritis is based on childhood memories of a long-suffering grandparent.

"Nobody can tell what the future holds, arthritis sufferers may have seen an elderly relative suffering terribly back when medicine wasn't as good [as it is now]," she says. In this situation, the best way to combat your fear is to articulate it, to find out the facts about your condition, and get a realistic prognosis. "Patients need to be able to express their fears and have accurate information, even if it isn't always good news," says Dr Williams. Even though there is no magic cure-all for arthritis, the fear of the unknown is almost always worse than the reality.

An important distinction must be made between different types of pain. Sometimes it is acute—when you stub your toe, or burn your finger—but with arthritis it is chronic. Acute pain is a warning mechanism, telling you to be careful when you walk, or to take your hand away from the flame, but this is not necessarily the case with chronic pain.

"People worry that if they push too much they will hasten their deterioration," says Dr Williams. But with arthritis the things that can hurt, especially exercises and stretching, are the very things that alleviate the pain in the long term. Talking to your doctor will give you the reassurance you need to differentiate between pain that is telling you to stop, and pain that is simply unavoidable.

Unfortunately for your GP, pain cannot

The Power of Positive Thinking

Dr Anna Mandeville is a clinical pyschologist in rheumatology, and has helped many arthritis sufferers learn to cope better with the chronic pain. She says that good pain management can help patients live a much more normal, enjoyable life. "Psychology plays a very important part," she says. "We can learn ways to manage pain so that we can continue with daily activities." Keeping a positive frame of mind is essential. "When faced with a challenging situation, it's common for us to produce negative thoughts," says Dr Mandeville. "This may lead us to staying at home, feeling at the mercy of the disease."

Dr Mandeville says that arthritis sufferers must learn to recognize negative thoughts, and replace them with more helpful ones. Instead of being sure you are too tired to do anything, for example, look at the things you had planned for the day, and try doing one or two of them at a pace you can manage.

Feeling in control of your condition helps you maintain a positive outlook. "Research shows that people who do best are those who are able to form a partnership with their healthcare team, and feel that they can take positive action in the face of chronic pain," says Dr Mandeville. This means that your GP or nurse takes the time to understand your specific concerns, and together you develop strategies to solve them. Arthritis cannot be cured, but with the right combination of medication and pain management, it can be controlled.

Get some faith

Having daily spiritual rituals or experiences may help some people with chronic pain feel better, suggests a study from Duke University in the USA. Every day for a month, 35 people with rheumatoid arthritis kept specially designed diaries, which contained questionnaires that rated their religious coping strategies, pain levels, mood, and social support.

"We found that people who felt that religious and spiritual coping strategies worked for them personally demonstrated that they really had less pain, better moods, and more social support," says Dr Francis Keefe, the director of the research. This study is one of the first to look at the immediate effects of everyday spiritual experiences. The diaries of those in the study revealed the following findings among other things.

Faith need not be formal

People in the study were more likely to say that they simply felt spiritually touched by the beauty of creation, they desired to be closer to, or in union with, God, they felt God's love directly or through others.

Positive faith works more effectively

People who looked to God for strength, support, and guidance fared better than people who wondered whether their illness was a sign that God was punishing them or had abandoned them.

Faith promoted better relationships

People who reported more frequent spiritual experiences also perceived more social support in their life.

---

be quantified like blood pressure or weight. That means you have to be able to explain what you are feeling so that he or she can give you the best advice and treatment. The same goes for friends, family and other healthcare professionals—they can't see a bruise or a swelling, so they can't judge how bad your pain is unless you tell them.

"Patients need to communicate, they need practical help and comfort," says Dr Williams. "Help is often given with the best of intentions, but for the patient it can be belittling. They need to be able to say 'no, I'll do it myself' and then five minutes later change their mind and ask for help." Sometimes families manage to resolve all the practical issues that are brought about by arthritis, but struggle to come to terms with the effects of the disease on the sufferer themselves. If it is difficult to change gear in the car because of stiff fingers or wrists, you can get an automatic, and the problem is simply solved. But if it hurts just getting out of bed in the morning, there is no quick fix.

"It's staggering – we see couples who have sorted out finances, child-care, but can't sort out the pain," says Dr Williams. She knows that for carers, it can be a source of unending frustration. Anxious to help, they can find themselves rebuffed at every turn.

"One of the things we hear most often is that they can't do anything right," she says. Relationships can be hard enough, without the added pressure of a long-term health problem like arthritis. Time and again, it boils down to good, two-way communication. Patients need to feel in control of their condition and its treatment, and recognize that the people that care for them have their own needs too.

Even with the best support network in the world, you may reach a point where you feel that you need professional help to learn to cope with living with constant pain. Seeing a psychologist or counsellor can be of immense benefit, helping you to identify the ways you react to and deal with your pain, and how you can manage it more effectively. The first step is to speak to your GP and ask for a referral—the NHS may be able to arrange for you to have sessions with a clinical psychologist who specialises in helping people to live positively with a chronic disease.

Alternatively, the **British Psychologist Society** have a search facility on their website to find practitioners near you, at **www.bps.org.uk**. The **British Association for Counselling and Psychotherapy** also has a helpline (Tel: **0870 443 5252**) with staff on hand to help you find a local counsellor who can help, and an online directory of therapists on their website at **www.bacp.co.uk**.

The Expert Patients Programme

Two years ago, the NHS set up a new scheme to empower patients with chronic conditions to help themselves, and others with the same conditions. In line with the new 'patient-centred' philosophy in the healthcare system, the Expert Patients Programme is based on long-standing research, which shows that patients themselves are often the best people to ask how to manage their medical condition.

The EPP is a half-day per week, six-week long course run by voluntary tutors who are themselves living with a long-term health condition. Debby Monkhouse, who co-ordinates the EPP for the Greenwich Primary Care Trust in London says that this benefits everyone involved. "It can really help with the feeling of isolation felt by many sufferers."

Groups of 8 to 16 patients meet to discuss their experiences. Some 2000 people have attended courses since they began in May 2002. Patients learn to manage their pain and fatigue, improve self-esteem, and become more confident to discuss it with their doctors. "Everyone makes a weekly action plan, and the group helps them overcome barriers," explains Monkhouse. Once they have begun to self-manage their condition successfully, patients can expect to make 40% less visits to their GPs, much shorter stays in hospital, and fewer days off work because of illness.

Programmes are run in community, leisure and health centres around the country. To find out where your nearest course is held, call the national help line on **0845 6066040** or visit the website **www.expertpatients.nhs.uk**.

CHAPTER 17

Juvenile Arthritis

This debilitating disease can affect the young as well as the old

Arthritis is not just an old person's disease, nor is it simply an unavoidable part of ageing, like hair loss or deteriorating eyesight. One in a thousand British children have a form of arthritis—a similar number to those with diabetes. Fortunately, 60% of people diagnosed in childhood will "grow-out" of the disease, and will not suffer as adults.

Most children grow out of arthritis

You're not too young to start

It doesn't matter whether you are 7 or 77 arthritis is no excuse to avoid exercise. Activity is one of the key weapons in the battle against arthritis. Whatever your age, activity can help you turn stiffness and pain into strength and power in your bones, joints, and muscles. Children are likely to be more fearful of exercising than adults, offer them support and encouragement and as with all exercise programmes start gently and build up slowly.

The most common form of arthritis in young people is oligoarthritis, a type that is particularly prevalent in girls under 5. It is also the mildest form of the disease, and with correct medication, physiotherapy, and other treatments, it should last no more than three or four years. Symptoms are stiff ankles, knees, and wrists, and an increased susceptibilty to uvetis, a condition that can, if left untreated, cause permanent damage to the eyes. It is essential that children with oligoarthritis go for regular eye check-ups.

Polyarthritis is also most common in girls. There are two types: rheumatoid factor (RF)-positive, and RF-negative. It affects the hands and feet, which makes writing and walking difficult. If a child is RF-positive then they will need early aggressive treatment to prevent serious joint damage, as they are likely to suffer from arthritis into adulthood.

One of the most difficult to diagnose types of arthritis is systemic arthritis, because its early symptoms are common to many childhood illnesses. An extremely high temperature, swollen glands, and a skin rash are the first signs, but doctors need to eliminate measles, leukaemia, and meningitis before they can confirm systemic arthritis.

Because it comes in bouts, children with systemic arthritis can go for long periods without problems, and often have only occasional "flare ups."

Both children and adults can suffer from psoriatic arthritis. It is easy to detect; sufferers will develop a scaly rash on their skin—their finger- and toe-nails will discolour—as well as joint pains, often in the fingers and toes. If a child has psoriatic arthritis he or she is also at risk of uvetis.

The only type of arthritis that is more common in boys than girls is enthesitis-related arthritis, which causes swelling at the points where bones and tendons are joined. It is often worse in the lower limbs, and increases the chances of a sufferer developing iritis, an eye condition similar to uvetis, so sufferers should again have regular eye check-ups.

Children with arthritis may feel very isolated, and that they are 'different' from their friends. Having arthritis can exacerbate the emotional turmoil of being a teenager, especially as taking steroids can delay the onset of puberty. While family and friends give as much love and support as they can, it can help for young people with arthritis to know there are others going through the same

Remember:

Pain in the wrists, hands, hips, or back will make sitting at a school desk difficult, and hospital appointments mean missed lessons. Talk to your head teacher, and to the school's Special Educational Needs Co-ordinator (SENCO) about your child's needs.

If your child is taking methotrexate or any other DMARD they should not have vaccinations for MMR, BCG, polio etc. Check with the doctor about immunisations.

Something as simple as teeth cleaning can be difficult for children with stiff, sore hands and wrist. Make sure they have regular dental check-ups and keep their teeth clean.

Exercise is absolutely essential for children with arthritis. They may not be able to do PE at school, but the exercises given by physiotherapists are very important.

things. **The Children's Chronic Arthritis Association (CCAA)** offers advice and support for children with arthritis and their families, and can be contacted on **01905 745595** or at **www.ccaa.org.uk**. **Arthritis Care** has a special helpline for people aged under 25 who either have arthritis, or help look after someone else who has it. It's a totally free, confidential service, on **0808 808 2000** and is manned during the week from 10am-2pm.

Pregnancy

Of the many types of arthritis, there are only two that cause any direct complications during pregnancy: rheumatoid arthritis and systemic lupus erythematosus.

If you suffer from RA, it's highly likely that you will actually find your symptoms lessen during pregnancy. It's a win-win situation; your health improves, and you need less medication, which is better for your baby. For expectant mothers with RA, it is the medication, rather than the disease itself, that is the risk. Non-steroidal anti-inflammatories, even aspirin, can cause bleeding of the placenta and prolong labour.

If you use other drugs, especially methotrexate, your doctor is likely to recommend that you stop taking them in the period leading up to and during your pregnancy, as it increases the risk of birth defects and miscarriage. This goes for prospective fathers too. That's why it's essential that if either of you have arthritis that you consult your doctor when you decide you want to start a family. Because so many new arthritis drugs are being introduced, there is not yet a substantial body of evidence to show the clear consequences of taking them either before conception or during pregnancy. Different drugs remain in your system for varying lengths of time, so you may need to come off your medication up to three months before you try to conceive, and not start taking them again until you have stopped breast-feeding. The usual advice about taking folic acid, giving up smoking, and cutting down on alcohol consumption still applies, too.

If you have arthritis in your knees, feet, or hips, the weight you gain as your baby grows inside you will put additional strain on your joints. But if your weight remains too low it could mean that either you or your baby aren't getting sufficient nutrients, so pay careful attention to your diet.

Perhaps the biggest fear that a parent-to-

Pregnancy Planning

Pregnancy and childbirth disrupt anyone's life, but the implications are greater for a woman with arthritis. You have to plan ahead more than someone without the condition. You need to address how your medication will affect your unborn child, what the implications are for you if you stop the medication, and how you are going to care for your child after it is born. For more information on arthritis and pregnancy, go to The Arthritis Foundation website: **www.arthritis.org.**

be will have is that their baby will develop arthritis. Most types of arthritis are not passed from parent to child—other factors such as age, weight, and joint injury play a much bigger role. Of the more common forms of arthritis, ankylosing spondylitis (AS) is the only one that is most likely to be passed on. If you have AS, and also have a certain blood cell type—human leucocyte antigen B27, or HLA-B27, which predisposes you to have AS—there is a one in six chance that your child will develop AS too.

For women with systemic lupus erythematosus, going through pregnancy can be extremely complicated, as it puts extra strain on your heart, lungs, and kidneys. There is an increased risk of your baby being born prematurely, being underweight, or having a condition called congenital heart block. It is also possible that your newborn child could have neo-natal lupus, although this usually disappears within the first few months after he or she is born. To minimize the

risks to yourself and your baby you should try to plan your pregnancy when you are in remission.

Whatever your particular circumstances, it is important to maintain the dialogue between your GP, your obstetrician and your rheumatologist. That way everyone will be able to monitor your pregnancy as it progresses. Pregnancy can be a difficult experience for all mums-to-be, but with careful planning there is no reason why you can't have a happy, healthy baby.

Most forms of arthritis aren't hereditary

CHAPTER 18

Know Your Rights

Understand the law and prevent arthritis being socially as well as physically debilitating

I f your arthritis incapacitates you in any way, either at home or in your ability to work, you may be entitled to claim financial benefits. The amount you can claim will depend on three things: your needs, your income, and, for some benefits, the amount you have contributed in National Insurance payments. These are the benefits that arthritis sufferers are most likely to be eligible for:

Incapacity Benefit. Payable if you are not able to work. Eligibility depends on National Insurance contributions made, and a medical examination to assess your level of incapacity.

Disability Living Allowance. There are two components to the DLA: one for care, one for mobility. Both parts are awarded at different levels, depending on the need of the individual. If your claim begins after the age of 65, you will get an Attendance Allowance. Neither of these allowances is means tested.

There are many other benefits that are not specifically for people with disabilities, but that you may qualify for if your arthritis limits your ability to work. These include Income Support (with a disability premium), Job Seeker's Allowance if you don't qualify for Incapacity Benefit, Disabled Person's Tax Credit, Housing Benefit, and Council Tax Benefit. If a friend or family member cares for you, they may be eligible for Invalid Carer's Allowance. You may also be eligible for free prescriptions, dental treatment, glasses, or contact lenses.

Employment

Although the Disability Discrimination Act was passed in 1995, it will not be fully implemented until October of this year. However, the part of the legislation relating to employment has been in place since 1996, so if you work for a company employing 15 people or more, it applies to you.

The Act states that you must not be discriminated against on the basis of your disability, unless your employer can show clear justification: that is, if you cannot safely and competently carry out the duties that a job entails. This covers the recruiting process, training, promotion, and dismissal. If you become disabled whilst in employment, or start a new job when you are disabled, your employer must make "reasonable adjustments" to your workplace to make it as easy as possible for you to carry out your duties by, for example, giving you an ergonomic chair or keyboard. These adjustments could also include improving access, allowing you to work more flexible hours, or changing jobs within the company, and, of course, allowing you time off for treatment.

Some unions have negotiated for "disabil-ity leave" for their members in the event of them becoming disabled. The Transport and General Workers' Union defines disability leave as time off for the employee and their family to learn to cope with their new situation—contact your own union to find out what your specific rights are.

Driving

As an arthritis sufferer it is likely that you will be dependent on your car, whether to get to and from hospital and doctor's appointments, or to make everyday journeys which are difficult to do by public transport or on foot.

By law, if you have a medical condition that lasts for three months or more, and it affects your driving, you must contact the Drivers' Medical Unit at the Driver & Vehicle Licensing Agency (DVLA) in Swansea and let them know about your condition. Contact the Medical Unit on **0870 600 0301**—when you call them they will ask some preliminary questions about your health so they know which forms to send you. If you do not drive when you are diagnosed, but subsequently begin driving lessons, you must make the DVLA aware of your arthritis when you apply for your provisional license. You will still have to pass the same theory and practical tests, but may be allowed extra time to do so.

The Queen Elizabeth's Foundation Mobility Centre in Surrey provides information, assessment, and tuition for drivers and learners alike. Contact them on **01372 841100** or visit **www.qefd.org**.

Don't forget that you must inform your insurance company about your condition too. They must not, by law, discriminate on the grounds of disability, so your premiums should not go up because of your arthritis.

CHAPTER 19

Easy Living Tips

A few simple changes can make all the difference in your day-to-day life

Even with good pain control, if your arthritis limits your mobility, flexibility or strength it can have a profound affect on your day-to-day living. Of course you want to maintain your independence, and to carry on with all the things you enjoyed doing before your diagnosis, and, with careful planning you can do just that. The most important thing is to listen to your body, accept help from friends and family when you want to.

You can still carry on with most chores provided you plan ahead

Sit up straight

You spend a lot of your time sitting down during a day, either in an office or at home. Sitting incorrectly can put a greater strain on your muscles, tendons and ligaments. In an office, make sure your chair is the right height for your work station – your arms should remain flexible and free with your feet firmly on the floor – to avoid slouching down or back and collapsing your spine. Your eyes are often a good indicator of whether you are sitting correctly, if you are straining your eyes you are probably straining your body too.

There are devices you can use in the kitchen, the bathroom and the garden to make everyday tasks easier. Many of them are so neat you'll find that the rest of your household wants to take advantage of them too. And they don't have to be expensive or complicated to use: you can save time and effort with simple, cleverly designed products, or just by using things you have at home in a new way. Here are a selection of some of the best easy living tips:

1 Ease strain on a bad back by using things with specially adapted long handles: dustpan and brush sets, shoe horns, and back-scrubbers with extended reach all save bending and twisting.

2 If you find it difficult to grip a knife with your fingers, use a pizza-wheel to cut toast and sandwiches.

3 Use liquid soaps, shower gels, shampoos, toothpastes and moisturers in pump dispensers, so you use the heel of your hand to operate them. It's less messy than using bars

of soap, and saves screwing lids on and off with each use.

4 Make dusting easier by swapping your cleaning cloth for an old sock. Slide it over your hand and wipe over surfaces with your palm, and into corners with your fingers.

5 To make getting in and out of the car much easier, use a strap of strong material, wind down the window and wrap one end around the top of the frame. Make a loop in the other end and use it as a handle to help take the weight off your feet as you bend.

6 Elastic shoe laces save bending down and dextrous finger movements. Available from shoe shops and sports shops — triathletes use them to change quickly in between the cycling and running legs of their races!

7 Swap your precision chopping knife for a rocker knife, either one that has a curved blade and needs less force to cut with, or one with a double handle that you can grip easily with both hands.

Arthritis and the bedroom

Arthritis doesn't have to lead to trouble in the bed

8 When you are doing jobs around the house or the garden, wear a carpenter's apron or belt to keep tools in. That way you won't be constantly wondering where you put something and going back to hunt for it.

9 If you find using zips on your trousers fiddly, thread on a key ring or a safety pin to give you something easier to grip. On cardigans or bags use a piece of ribbon to make an attractive detail.

10 Install a second handrail on the wall going up the stairs. You can also put up rails in the bathroom by the tub and by the side of the toilet.

11 Get a 'reaching stick' or 'grabber' to pick things up off the floor, get clothes in and out of a front-loading washing machine, or to reach up to things on high shelves.

12 Take the wire basket from a deep-fat fryer and use it in a saucepan when you

For all of us, there are two important activities that normally happen in the bedroom: sleep and sex. Both are likely to be affected by arthritis.

Being in pain or discomfort will have an immediate impact on your ability to sleep, and a bad night's sleep will inevitably lead to a difficult day. Following the correct medical, dietary, and exercise advice can alleviate the physical symptoms that interfere with your sleep patterns.

You also need to pay attention to your sleeping position. Most people sleep in the foetal position, which isn't a problem as long as the bed offers support. If the mattress is too soft or you use too many pillows, you can put an unnecessary strain on your spine and your neck. Aim to keep your spine horizontal and straight.

Many of the issues concerning arthritis and sexual relationships are not particular to your medical condition. Feeling tired, unattractive, or unhappy with other aspects of your relationship—particularly if you have become financially or physically dependent on your partner—can, and does, happen to everyone. It's more important than ever that you communicate with your partner in bed, to avoid doing anything that hurts your sensitive joints, and to make sure you both get as much pleasure from the relationship as you did before you had arthritis.

It's unlikely that you'll feel like swinging from the chandelier when your hip is flaring up, but there are plenty of ways to be intimate without a display of bedroom gymnastics. Experiment with different positions to find ways of enjoying yourselves without putting strain on your joints. Both lying on your sides, with the woman in front of the man, is a good place to start. If either of you have hip or knee problems it may be easiest to lie underneath your partner, with their legs outside of yours (it works both ways), with a pillow under the hips if necessary. If it's painful to kneel, you can stand up and lean against the furniture. Of course, you don't have to have penetrative sex, you can stimulate one another, or yourself, in other ways. Just remember communication and imagination are more important than ever!

are cooking vegetables or pasta. That way you won't have to carry a heavy pan of boiling water across to the sink to drain them, saving effort and avoiding a possible spill.

13 Purchase a wrist rest to take the strain off your wrists when you use a computer. You can make your own with two strips of bubble wrap packing material taped together.

14 To make heavy loads easier to move and carry, use your largest and strongest joints and muscles to take the strain off smaller hand joints and to spread the effort. Slide objects rather than lifting them and hold items close to your body, which is less stressful for your joints.

15 When joints are hot and inflamed, applying something cold such as a pack of frozen peas, can decrease the pain and swelling by constricting blood vessels and preventing fluids from leaking into surrounding tissues.

CHAPTER 20

Sneak Some Exercise Into Your Life

You can incorportate some exercise into every day without even realizing it

The idea of exercising to help improve your condition can seem daunting—especially if you are experiencing pain or have taken little physical activity since your diagnosis. Add to that the fact that many of us are pressed for time and modern life is full of gadgets designed to make life less physically demanding, and it's little wonder that most of the population—let alone arthritis sufferers—don't get enough exercise.

But exercising doesn't have to mean Lycra and expensive gym memberships. Incorporating exercise into everyday life is surprisingly easy. Here are tips to make every day an exercise in itself.

Your remote could be harming your health

Dump the gadgets

Television remote controls and e-mail have a lot to answer for. Of course, changing the TV channels manually isn't the equivalent of a marathon, but getting up from the sofa and switching soaps burns a few extra calories and stretches muscles and joints that sitting on the sofa doesn't. And the same goes for strolling around to the accounts department rather than sending an e-mail.

Decline a lift

You might want to ignore this advice if you work at the top of Canary Wharf, but if your office—or favourite shop—is up a few flights of stairs, then use them rather than the lift or escalator. It doesn't sound like much, but walking up and down a couple of flights a day adds up to plenty of extra calories burned and muscles strengthened over a year.

Walk, don't drive

The car is our most obvious excuse for not exercising, so every now and again try and do without it or at least limit its use. Take a stroll down to the newsagents, or park in the car park furthest from the shops.

Sit down to work out

Even if you're not up and about you can exercise. At your desk or in the car you can stretch out and loosen aching muscles and joints. For example, when you're sitting in traffic simply tighten your stomach, hold for a few seconds and release—a tiny movement but it builds strength. Or grip the steering wheel and push back gently into your seat for a simple strengthening routine.

TAKE CONTROL

Learn stationary stretching

Keep moving when at your desk, stuck at traffic lights or watching television. Try a few simple exercises. Pushing your head against cupped hands; forcing your hands together with elbows bent or tightening your buttock muscles while seated are a few easy ways to stay active.

Clean up

Household chores might not be exciting, but they count as exercise. Washing dishes in warm water can actually help soothe sore joints, as can wringing out the dish cloth, and scrubbing plates is a good stretch for fingers. Even if you use a dishwasher, you can use it to your advantage—gently bending to take out the cutlery can stretch your leg and back muscles. Then there's vacuuming—this uses both arm and leg muscles, and if you do it vigorously you can even work up a sweat. And on a sunny day, wash your car. Big circular movements with the sponge provide a good range of movement for stiff wrists and arms.

Get green fingered

Gardening is a great all-round exercise—it stretches muscles, loosens joints, and builds strength. Practical tasks such as mowing the lawn, pulling up weeds, digging up earth, and sweeping away leaves are all top ways to exercise.

the arthritis action plan

The best way to take on arthritis is one day at a time

CHAPTER 21

Beat Arthritis In 30 Days

Reduce pain, get stronger, and feel great —starting today!

When it comes to arthritis, it's best to take one day at a time. And with this 30-day planner, each day will open up a world of information for you to take control of your arthritis for good.

With each new day, you'll learn three tips about eating, exercise, and arthritis care. By the end of the month, you'll have an arsenal of 90 simple solutions to all your arthritis concerns.

The daily checklist will help you keep track of your joint-saving eating plan (Chapter 8) as well as your walking programme (Chapter 12) and pain-reducing fitness programme (Chapter 14). You also have room to jot down how you're feeling, so you can spot trends and identify what works for you.

You have the power to stop arthritis pain and live an active life. Go ahead and start today!

**Swing into a new
pain-free life**

DAY 1

eat right!
Dress up your salmon

Fish rich in omega-3 fatty acids, such as salmon, helps fight arthritis inflammation. Make healthy taste fabulous with this quick glaze: in a small saucepan over medium-high heat, bring 50 ml each of orange juice and maple syrup and 3 tablespoons of balsamic vinegar to a simmer. Cook the mix until it's reduced to about 4 tablespoons. Brush this glaze on the fish while broiling.

keep moving!
Take yoga for arthritis

Yoga will help you improve your range of motion, muscle strength, and endurance—three key goals for exercise programmes for people with arthritis. Many yoga centres have classes specially tailored for arthritis sufferers, and if they don't, they will help you modify routines to suit you. To find an accredited teacher near you, contact the **British Wheel of Yoga** at **www.bwy.org.uk**, or phone them on **01529 306851**.

feel great!
Turn on the heat

No more "it hurts too much to walk in the morning!" Use an electric blanket or mattress pad. Turn it on before you get out of bed in the morning to melt away that morning stiffness.

CHECKLIST

(See p62 for your strong-joints eating plan.)

FOOD

Water (8 or more servings)
☐ ☐ ☐ ☐ ☐ ☐ ☐ ☐

Vegetables (3 or more servings)
☐ ☐ ☐

Fruits (3 or more servings)
☐ ☐ ☐

Grains (4 to 9 servings)
(at least half from wholegrains)
☐ ☐ ☐ ☐ ☐ ☐ ☐ ☐ ☐

Fish, soya, nuts & legumes
(1 or more servings) ☐

Milk, yoghurt & cheese
(2 or 3 servings) ☐ ☐ ☐

Meat, poultry & eggs
(2 or less servings) ☐ ☐

SUPPLEMENTS

Multivitamin/mineral ☐
with 100% of RNI for most nutrients

Vitamin D: 10 mcg ☐
(only recommended if you are over 65. Try not to exceed 25 mcg per day as high levels reaching 50 mcg can be dangerous)

Vitamin E:
Discuss dosage with your doctor ☐

ACTIVITY DIARY

☐ I walked ___ minutes, ___ miles, or ___ steps *(p. 106)*

☐ I did the "Get Fit, Firm and Pain Free!" workout *(p. 118)*

HOW I FEEL TODAY *(0 = very bad, 10 = very good)*

Pain Scale _____, Mobility/physical ability scale_____

OTHER COMMENTS *(Strategies that worked, inflammation triggers, medication notes or reminders, doctors' appointments, etc.)*

_____

_____

_____

_____

DAY 2

eat right!
Stop pain with produce

Research has shown that people with high intakes of vitamin C and beta-carotene have a reduced risk of knee pain and arthritis progression. To be sure that you get enough of these nutrients (as well as other plant-based protective compounds, such as lutein and lycopene), eat lots of carrots, sweet potatoes, broccoli, spinach, tomato sauce and tomato juice, oranges, kiwi fruit, and strawberries.

keep moving!
Walk the walk

Walking is an ideal exercise for people with arthritis. Take time to explore where you live on foot— you'll be surprised at how much you miss in the car. Or get your family involved in a Walk For Arthritis fundraiser. The **Arthritis Research Campaign** organize sponsored walks around the UK—call them on **0870 850 5000** for details.

feel great!
Soothe achy joints gingerly

A teaspoon of freshly grated ginger in a cup of boiling water may help beat arthritis pain, and makes a refreshing tea. Fill a Thermos in the morning, and sip away for all-day pain relief.

CHECKLIST

(See p62 for your strong-joints eating plan.)

FOOD

Water (8 or more servings)
☐ ☐ ☐ ☐ ☐ ☐ ☐ ☐

Vegetables (3 or more servings)
☐ ☐ ☐

Fruits (3 or more servings)
☐ ☐ ☐

Grains (4 to 9 servings)
(at least half from wholegrains)
☐ ☐ ☐ ☐ ☐ ☐ ☐ ☐ ☐

Fish, soya, nuts & legumes
(1 or more servings) ☐

Milk, yoghurt & cheese
(2 or 3 servings) ☐ ☐ ☐

Meat, poultry & eggs
(2 or less servings) ☐ ☐

SUPPLEMENTS

Multivitamin/mineral ☐
with 100% of RNI for most nutrients

Vitamin D: 10 mcg ☐
(only recommended if you are over 65. Try not to exceed 25 mcg per day as high levels reaching 50 mcg can be dangerous)

Vitamin E:
Discuss dosage with your doctor ☐

ACTIVITY DIARY

☐ I walked ___ minutes, ___ miles, or ___ steps *(p. 106)*

☐ I did the "Get Fit, Firm and Pain Free!" workout *(p. 118)*

HOW I FEEL TODAY *(0 = very bad, 10 = very good)*

Pain Scale ____, Mobility/physical ability scale____

OTHER COMMENTS *(Strategies that worked, inflammation triggers, medication notes or reminders, doctors' appointments, etc.)*

_____

_____

_____

_____

_____

DAY 3

eat right!
Drink green tea every day

Green tea is rich in polyphenols, chemical compounds that appear to prevent inflammatory cells from getting into joints to do damage. Green tea is also rich in the antioxidant vitamins C and E, nutrients that "neutralize" joint-damaging molecules in the body called free radicals.

keep moving!
Stay seated

If you're experiencing a flare-up, have severe hip or knee damage, or balance problems, try exercising from a chair rather than not exercising at all.

feel great!
Computer type

If you use a computer, either at work or at home, make sure your desktop is set up properly. A wrist-rest will help keep your hands in a neutral positon, or you can swap your standard QWERTY keyboard for a split-design one. You can even get a differently-laid out DVORAK keyboard, with the most commonly used letters in the easiest-to-reach places (Mac computers have this as a built-in option), and a foot-operated mouse if your hands are too painful to use a normal one.

CHECKLIST

(See p62 for your strong-joints eating plan.)

FOOD

Water (8 or more servings)
☐ ☐ ☐ ☐ ☐ ☐ ☐ ☐

Vegetables (3 or more servings)
☐ ☐ ☐

Fruits (3 or more servings)
☐ ☐ ☐

Grains (4 to 9 servings)
(at least half from wholegrains)
☐ ☐ ☐ ☐ ☐ ☐ ☐ ☐ ☐

Fish, soya, nuts & legumes
(1 or more servings) ☐

Milk, yoghurt & cheese
(2 or 3 servings) ☐ ☐ ☐

Meat, poultry & eggs
(2 or less servings) ☐ ☐

SUPPLEMENTS

Multivitamin/mineral ☐
with 100% of RNI for most nutrients

Vitamin D: 10 mcg ☐
(only recommended if you are over 65. Try not to exceed 25 mcg per day as high levels reaching 50 mcg can be dangerous)

Vitamin E:
Discuss dosage with your doctor ☐

ACTIVITY DIARY

☐ I walked ___ minutes, ___ miles, or ___ steps *(p. 106)*

☐ I did the "Get Fit, Firm and Pain Free!" workout *(p. 118)*

HOW I FEEL TODAY *(0 = very bad, 10 = very good)*

Pain Scale ___, Mobility/physical ability scale___

OTHER COMMENTS *(Strategies that worked, inflammation triggers, medication notes or reminders, doctors' appointments, etc.)*

_____
_____
_____
_____
_____

DAY 4

eat right!
Try out a new oil

Flaxseed oil is a good source of linolenic acid or LNA, another anti-inflammatory omega-3 fatty acid. Include it in your daily diet in salad dressings, for example, or as an ingredient in recipes that don't involve heating. Store in the fridge.

keep moving!
Active recovery

Knee replacement surgery is no reason to give up exercise, according to a University of Pittsburgh study. Those who continued to walk, garden, and do other activities were no more likely to need a second operation than those who were sedentary. In fact, those who were more active were about one-third less likely to need to have surgery again. To safely resume exercise, talk to your doctor first.

feel great!
Read drug labels carefully

Are you taking the cyclosporin or cyclophosphamide? With so many medicines available, it's not difficult to get confused. Ask your doctor to include the brand and generic names on the prescription, along with the reason for use. This helps the pharmacist choose the right drug when it's time to fill the prescription. As always, read labels carefully before leaving the pharmacy.

CHECKLIST
(See p62 for your strong-joints eating plan.)

FOOD

Water (8 or more servings)
☐ ☐ ☐ ☐ ☐ ☐ ☐ ☐

Vegetables (3 or more servings)
☐ ☐ ☐

Fruits (3 or more servings)
☐ ☐ ☐

Grains (4 to 9 servings)
(at least half from wholegrains)
☐ ☐ ☐ ☐ ☐ ☐ ☐ ☐ ☐

Fish, soya, nuts & legumes
(1 or more servings) ☐

Milk, yoghurt & cheese
(2 or 3 servings) ☐ ☐ ☐

Meat, poultry & eggs
(2 or less servings) ☐ ☐

SUPPLEMENTS

Multivitamin/mineral ☐
with 100% of RNI for most nutrients

Vitamin D: 10 mcg ☐
(only recommended if you are over 65. Try not to exceed 25 mcg per day as high levels reaching 50 mcg can be dangerous)

Vitamin E:
Discuss dosage with your doctor ☐

ACTIVITY DIARY

☐ I walked ___ minutes, ___ miles, or ___ steps *(p. 106)*

☐ I did the "Get Fit, Firm and Pain Free!" workout *(p. 118)*

HOW I FEEL TODAY *(0 = very bad, 10 = very good)*

Pain Scale ___, Mobility/physical ability scale___

OTHER COMMENTS *(Strategies that worked, inflammation triggers, medication notes or reminders, doctors' appointments, etc.)*

_____
_____
_____
_____
_____

DAY 5

eat right!
How much should you eat?

To maintain your weight, find out how many calories you should consume in the chart below, based on your gender and current weight, assuming you're fairly sedentary. Go above that number and you'll gain, below it and you'll lose.

Calories:	1,867	2,294	2,010	2,535	2,153	2,776
Weight:	130 lb		160 lb		190 lb	

WOMAN: 50 years old, 5' tall. **MAN:** 50 years old, 5'10" tall
Source: Baylor College of Medicine, Houston

keep moving!
Pain-free workouts

Take an anti-inflammatory medication or over-the-counter pain reliever 30 minutes before you start your walk. Then warm up. **For your knees:** Sit in a chair, and slowly raise your left foot until your leg is straight. Hold for a second, then slowly lower. Repeat 10 to 15 times, then switch legs. **For your hips:** Lie on your back with your knees bent in towards your chest. Slowly move your knees in an ever-widening circle, keeping your lower spine on the floor. Do 10 times, then switch direction.

feel great!
Treat yourself to satin

Turning in a bed made with satin sheets will be slippery smooth, reducing nightly discomfort and ensuring a solid night's sleep. Indulge in a pair of satin pyjamas and you're almost guaranteed sweet dreams. Satin sheets are available from all major department stores.

CHECKLIST

(See p62 for your strong-joints eating plan.)

FOOD

Water (8 or more servings)
☐ ☐ ☐ ☐ ☐ ☐ ☐ ☐

Vegetables (3 or more servings)
☐ ☐ ☐

Fruits (3 or more servings)
☐ ☐ ☐

Grains (4 to 9 servings)
(at least half from wholegrains)
☐ ☐ ☐ ☐ ☐ ☐ ☐ ☐ ☐

Fish, soya, nuts & legumes
(1 or more servings) ☐

Milk, yoghurt & cheese
(2 or 3 servings) ☐ ☐ ☐

Meat, poultry & eggs
(2 or less servings) ☐ ☐

SUPPLEMENTS

Multivitamin/mineral ☐
with 100% of RNI for most nutrients

Vitamin D: 10 mcg ☐
(only recommended if you are over 65. Try not to exceed 25 mcg per day as high levels reaching 50 mcg can be dangerous)

Vitamin E:
Discuss dosage with your doctor ☐

ACTIVITY DIARY

☐ I walked ___ minutes, ___ miles, or ___ steps *(p. 106)*

☐ I did the "Get Fit, Firm and Pain Free!" workout *(p. 118)*

HOW I FEEL TODAY *(0 = very bad, 10 = very good)*

Pain Scale _____, Mobility/physical ability scale_____

OTHER COMMENTS *(Strategies that worked, inflammation triggers, medication notes or reminders, doctors' appointments, etc.)*

_____
_____
_____
_____
_____

DAY 6

eat right!
Eat more of these

To get more anti-inflammatory omega-3s, try:

- ▶ A tablespoon of ground flaxseed on breakfast cereal
- ▶ A handful of walnuts (10 halves) for a snack
- ▶ A salmon sandwich for lunch
- ▶ Omega-3–enriched eggs, available from all major supermarkets

keep moving!
Fight fibromyalgia

Slip away from pain—in a warm pool. In a Harvard Medical School study, women with fibromyalgia who walked and did muscle-strengthening exercises had less pain, stiffness, and fatigue. The secret: they began with gentle water routines. Water supports and soothes your body while you improve flexibility and strength. But look for a warm pool as exercising in cool water may make muscle pain worse.

feel great!
Don't put up with pain

If you can't seem to get any relief from the pain or joint swelling, ask your GP to refer you to a Pain Clinic. These clinics are for people with chronic pain, and have teams of doctors, psychologists, nurses, physiotherapists, occupational therapists who will help you learn to cope better. Many run courses for patients with similar problems, such as Pain Management Programmes, which are psychologically based schemes to reduce the impact pain has on your everyday life.

CHECKLIST

(See p62 for your strong-joints eating plan.)

FOOD

Water (8 or more servings)
☐ ☐ ☐ ☐ ☐ ☐ ☐ ☐

Vegetables (3 or more servings)
☐ ☐ ☐

Fruits (3 or more servings)
☐ ☐ ☐

Grains (4 to 9 servings)
(at least half from wholegrains)
☐ ☐ ☐ ☐ ☐ ☐ ☐ ☐ ☐

Fish, soya, nuts & legumes
(1 or more servings) ☐

Milk, yoghurt & cheese
(2 or 3 servings) ☐ ☐ ☐

Meat, poultry & eggs
(2 or less servings) ☐ ☐

SUPPLEMENTS

Multivitamin/mineral ☐
with 100% of RNI for most nutrients

Vitamin D: 10 mcg ☐
(only recommended if you are over 65. Try not to exceed 25 mcg per day as high levels reaching 50 mcg can be dangerous)

Vitamin E:
Discuss dosage with your doctor ☐

ACTIVITY DIARY

☐ I walked ___ minutes, ___ miles, or ___ steps *(p. 106)*

☐ I did the "Get Fit, Firm and Pain Free!" workout *(p. 118)*

HOW I FEEL TODAY *(0 = very bad, 10 = very good)*

Pain Scale ____, Mobility/physical ability scale____

OTHER COMMENTS *(Strategies that worked, inflammation triggers, medication notes or reminders, doctors' appointments, etc.)*

_____

_____

_____

_____

_____

DAY 7

eat right!
Mend with methotrexate

Methotrexate is used to treat RA. It competes with folic acid for specific binding sites within the body because it has a similar structure to folic acid. Doctors may prescribe folic acid supplements to compensate. If you're taking methotrexate, it's a good idea to get plenty of folic acid in your diet through produce, fortified cereals and grains.

keep moving!
Strengthen your hips

Weak and tight hips go hand in hand. Try this stretch, holding for 20 seconds. Lie on your back with your knees

bent and your feet flat on the floor, arms by your side. Cross your right ankle over your left knee so that your right shin is parallel to the floor. Slowly drop your legs to the left, bringing your right foot down towards the floor as far as comfortably possible. Gently press against your right knee with your left hand. Hold, then switch sides.

feel great!
A user-friendly kitchen

An organized kitchen is a sure-fire way to reduce arthritis pain. Try roll-out baskets in low-level cupboards, step-up shelf extenders, wire dividers in drawers, easy-to-grip kitchen tools. Make food preparation as easy as possible: use a salad spinner, electric can-opener, a garlic press.

CHECKLIST
(See p62 for your strong-joints eating plan.)

FOOD

Water (8 or more servings)
☐ ☐ ☐ ☐ ☐ ☐ ☐ ☐

Vegetables (3 or more servings)
☐ ☐ ☐

Fruits (3 or more servings)
☐ ☐ ☐

Grains (4 to 9 servings)
(at least half from wholegrains)
☐ ☐ ☐ ☐ ☐ ☐ ☐ ☐ ☐

Fish, soya, nuts & legumes
(1 or more servings) ☐

Milk, yoghurt & cheese
(2 or 3 servings) ☐ ☐ ☐

Meat, poultry & eggs
(2 or less servings) ☐ ☐

SUPPLEMENTS

Multivitamin/mineral ☐
with 100% of RNI for most nutrients

Vitamin D: 10 mcg ☐
(only recommended if you are over 65. Try not to exceed 25 mcg per day as high levels reaching 50 mcg can be dangerous)

Vitamin E:
Discuss dosage with your doctor ☐

ACTIVITY DIARY

☐ I walked ___ minutes, ___ miles, or ___ steps *(p. 106)*

☐ I did the "Get Fit, Firm and Pain Free!" workout *(p. 118)*

HOW I FEEL TODAY *(0 = very bad, 10 = very good)*

Pain Scale ____, Mobility/physical ability scale____

OTHER COMMENTS *(Strategies that worked, inflammation triggers, medication notes or reminders, doctors' appointments, etc.)*

_____

_____

_____

_____

DAY 8

eat right!
A life-saving fashion tip

Can't figure out how you're going to remember to eat all those fruits and vegetables in a day? Buy yourself six or more beaded or bangle bracelets. Every morning, place all the bracelets on one wrist. Then move one bracelet to your other wrist each time you eat a fruit or vegetable. Make sure all the bracelets have been moved by the end of the day. It's that simple!

keep moving!
Soothing sounds

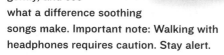

Music acts as an analgesic that helps people with arthritis and other chronic pain to get moving. Start gently, and see what a difference soothing songs make. Important note: Walking with headphones requires caution. Stay alert.

feel great!
Shoe swap

Wide high heels may feel comfortable and seem safe, but research says they can cause even more damage to your knees than spiky high heels. Many women wear wide heels for longer periods of time and walk longer distances in them than they would in skinny heels. It is not yet known how high is too high, but one thing is for sure: The less time you spend in any heels, the better.

CHECKLIST
(See p62 for your strong-joints eating plan.)

FOOD

Water (8 or more servings)
☐ ☐ ☐ ☐ ☐ ☐ ☐ ☐

Vegetables (3 or more servings)
☐ ☐ ☐

Fruits (3 or more servings)
☐ ☐ ☐

Grains (4 to 9 servings)
(at least half from wholegrains)
☐ ☐ ☐ ☐ ☐ ☐ ☐ ☐ ☐

Fish, soya, nuts & legumes
(1 or more servings) ☐

Milk, yoghurt & cheese
(2 or 3 servings) ☐ ☐ ☐

Meat, poultry & eggs
(2 or less servings) ☐ ☐

SUPPLEMENTS

Multivitamin/mineral ☐
with 100% of RNI for most nutrients

Vitamin D: 10 mcg ☐
(only recommended if you are over 65. Try not to exceed 25 mcg per day as high levels reaching 50 mcg can be dangerous)

Vitamin E:
Discuss dosage with your doctor ☐

ACTIVITY DIARY

☐ I walked ___ minutes, ___ miles, or ___ steps *(p. 106)*

☐ I did the "Get Fit, Firm and Pain Free!" workout *(p. 118)*

HOW I FEEL TODAY *(0 = very bad, 10 = very good)*

Pain Scale ___, Mobility/physical ability scale___

OTHER COMMENTS *(Strategies that worked, inflammation triggers, medication notes or reminders, doctors' appointments, etc.)*

_____

_____

_____

_____

_____

DAY 9

eat right!
Take vitamin E with meals

Absorb more vitamin E by taking it with a meal. Research subjects who took vitamin E supplements with a fat-containing meal absorbed three times as much as those who took it on an empty stomach. Their antioxidant protection increased by 14%, while the empty-tummy group had no increase.

keep moving!
Step away from the paper!

Scrap just 2 minutes from reading the morning paper in favour of doing two sets of crunches. Five fewer minutes scanning e-mails or the *Radio Times* buys you time for stairclimbing and lunges. Shave 10 minutes off your lunch break, and go for a walk. Each week, subtract another inactive minute or two, until you're in motion for 10, 15, even 20 minutes.

feel great!
Make a stand

Take a stand for people with arthritis. Write to your MP to ask for patients to be given better access to treatment across the country. **Arthritis Care** run campaigns – visit **www.arthritiscare.org.uk/campaigns** to find out more. Arthritis Care's Awareness Week is April 25-30 this year, so contact them on **0808 800 4050** to find out how you can get involved.

CHECKLIST
(See p62 for your strong-joints eating plan.)

FOOD

Water (8 or more servings)
☐ ☐ ☐ ☐ ☐ ☐ ☐ ☐

Vegetables (3 or more servings)
☐ ☐ ☐

Fruits (3 or more servings)
☐ ☐ ☐

Grains (4 to 9 servings)
(at least half from wholegrains)
☐ ☐ ☐ ☐ ☐ ☐ ☐ ☐ ☐

Fish, soya, nuts & legumes
(1 or more servings) ☐

Milk, yoghurt & cheese
(2 or 3 servings) ☐ ☐ ☐

Meat, poultry & eggs
(2 or less servings) ☐ ☐

SUPPLEMENTS

Multivitamin/mineral ☐
with 100% of RNI for most nutrients

Vitamin D: 10 mcg ☐
(only recommended if you are over 65. Try not to exceed 25 mcg per day as high levels reaching 50 mcg can be dangerous)

Vitamin E:
Discuss dosage with your doctor ☐

ACTIVITY DIARY

☐ I walked ___ minutes, ___ miles, or ___ steps *(p. 106)*

☐ I did the "Get Fit, Firm and Pain Free!" workout *(p. 118)*

HOW I FEEL TODAY *(0 = very bad, 10 = very good)*

Pain Scale ____, Mobility/physical ability scale____

OTHER COMMENTS *(Strategies that worked, inflammation triggers, medication notes or reminders, doctors' appointments, etc.)*

_____
_____
_____
_____
_____

DAY 10

eat right!

Fresh – and fast – matchstick carrots

Here's a tasty beta-carotene-rich side dish that's ready in just 4 minutes: buy a bag of pre-cut matchstick carrots. Take 250 g and pop them in the microwave for 4 minutes. Add 2 teaspoons of apricot jam to make them divine for about 90 calories total—and 5 g of fibre!

keep moving!

Listen to your body

Stop if you experience sharp, shooting, or stabbing pain; if the pain gets worse over time; if it doesn't go away; or if there is swelling or redness of the joint. Ice arthritic joints for about 20 minutes if you experience an increase in pain or swelling.

feel great!

Give yourself a warm-water treat

Applying heat to sore joints can be very soothing, especially in the morning, when joints are stiffest. The easiest way to heat the joints is to have a hot bath or shower. Or, using warm water (not above 90°F), you can moisten a towel or fill up a hot-water bottle and hold it to the affected area. When the towel or hot-water bottle cools, wet or fill it up again and repeat the treatment.

CHECKLIST

(See p62 for your strong-joints eating plan.)

FOOD

Water (8 or more servings)
☐ ☐ ☐ ☐ ☐ ☐ ☐ ☐

Vegetables (3 or more servings)
☐ ☐ ☐

Fruits (3 or more servings)
☐ ☐ ☐

Grains (4 to 9 servings)
(at least half from wholegrains)
☐ ☐ ☐ ☐ ☐ ☐ ☐ ☐ ☐

Fish, soya, nuts & legumes
(1 or more servings) ☐

Milk, yoghurt & cheese
(2 or 3 servings) ☐ ☐ ☐

Meat, poultry & eggs
(2 or less servings) ☐ ☐

SUPPLEMENTS

Multivitamin/mineral ☐
with 100% of RNI for most nutrients

Vitamin D: 10 mcg ☐
(only recommended if you are over 65. Try not to exceed 25 mcg per day as high levels reaching 50 mcg can be dangerous)

Vitamin E:
Discuss dosage with your doctor ☐

ACTIVITY DIARY

☐ I walked ___ minutes, ___ miles, or ___ steps *(p. 106)*

☐ I did the "Get Fit, Firm and Pain Free!" workout *(p. 118)*

HOW I FEEL TODAY *(0 = very bad, 10 = very good)*

Pain Scale ___, Mobility/physical ability scale___

OTHER COMMENTS *(Strategies that worked, inflammation triggers, medication notes or reminders, doctors' appointments, etc.)*

_____

_____

_____

_____

_____

DAY 11

eat right!
Drink up!

Water is an essential part of your strong-joint nutritional programme. To make sure you get your eight or more glasses a day, try these tips:

▶ Sip water while you make the morning coffee. After a night's sleep, your body is at its most dehydrated.

▶ Fill a water bottle at home. Carry it in your car, and put it on your desk. It's convenient, and a visual reminder to drink.

keep moving!
Take 10

Don't feel like exercising today? Set your watch alarm or minute timer for 10 minutes at the start of your walk or aerobics video. If you want to quit after 10 minutes, go ahead. Chances are, you'll feel so good, you'll keep going.

feel great!
Spa treatment

If you're having trouble with joints in the hands or feet, you may want to try a "paraffin bath," in which the joints are coated with a warm, waxy coating to deliver long-lasting heat to relieve stiffness and pain. The treatment is available at beauticians, nail salons and health spas nationwide.

CHECKLIST

(See p62 for your strong-joints eating plan.)

FOOD

Water (8 or more servings)
☐ ☐ ☐ ☐ ☐ ☐ ☐ ☐

Vegetables (3 or more servings)
☐ ☐ ☐

Fruits (3 or more servings)
☐ ☐ ☐

Grains (4 to 9 servings)
(at least half from wholegrains)
☐ ☐ ☐ ☐ ☐ ☐ ☐ ☐ ☐

Fish, soya, nuts & legumes
(1 or more servings) ☐

Milk, yoghurt & cheese
(2 or 3 servings) ☐ ☐ ☐

Meat, poultry & eggs
(2 or less servings) ☐ ☐

SUPPLEMENTS

Multivitamin/mineral ☐
with 100% of RNI for most nutrients

Vitamin D: 10 mcg ☐
(only recommended if you are over 65. Try not to exceed 25 mcg per day as high levels reaching 50 mcg can be dangerous)

Vitamin E:
Discuss dosage with your doctor ☐

ACTIVITY DIARY

☐ I walked ___ minutes, ___ miles, or ___ steps *(p. 106)*

☐ I did the "Get Fit, Firm and Pain Free!" workout *(p. 118)*

HOW I FEEL TODAY *(0 = very bad, 10 = very good)*

Pain Scale _____, Mobility/physical ability scale_____

OTHER COMMENTS *(Strategies that worked, inflammation triggers, medication notes or reminders, doctors' appointments, etc.)*

_____
_____
_____
_____
_____

DAY 12

eat right!
A chore no more

Are vegetables too much work? Not after these time-saving tips.

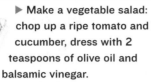

▶ Use frozen vegetables. Steam, microwave, or sauté them in olive oil with a little garlic.

▶ Make a vegetable salad: chop up a ripe tomato and cucumber, dress with 2 teaspoons of olive oil and balsamic vinegar.

▶ Buy pre-washed and peeled baby carrots, grape tomatoes, and chopped cauliflower and broccoli.

keep moving!
Walking power

This easy move will help you walk further and faster.
Toe Walk (strengthens calves): Walk on the balls of your feet, heels off the floor, for 30 seconds. Repeat three times.

feel great!
Breathe away pain

In Traditional Chinese Medicine, some believe arthritis is often caused by a combination of factors that includes a blockage of chi, usually caused by tension or stress. A special type of breathing called Hara builds reserves of chi in your body. To give it a try, place your hand, palm down, right below your navel. Next, inhale, expanding your belly into your hand. Imagine breathing vitality down into your belly with the breaths, and concentrating it there as you exhale, feeling your belly flatten.

CHECKLIST

(See p62 for your strong-joints eating plan.)

FOOD

Water (8 or more servings)
☐ ☐ ☐ ☐ ☐ ☐ ☐ ☐

Vegetables (3 or more servings)
☐ ☐ ☐

Fruits (3 or more servings)
☐ ☐ ☐

Grains (4 to 9 servings)
(at least half from wholegrains)
☐ ☐ ☐ ☐ ☐ ☐ ☐ ☐ ☐

Fish, soya, nuts & legumes
(1 or more servings) ☐

Milk, yoghurt & cheese
(2 or 3 servings) ☐ ☐ ☐

Meat, poultry & eggs
(2 or less servings) ☐ ☐

SUPPLEMENTS

Multivitamin/mineral ☐
with 100% of RNI for most nutrients

Vitamin D: 10 mcg ☐
(only recommended if you are over 65. Try not to exceed 25 mcg per day as high levels reaching 50 mcg can be dangerous)

Vitamin E:
Discuss dosage with your doctor ☐

ACTIVITY DIARY

☐ I walked ___ minutes, ___ miles, or ___ steps *(p. 106)*

☐ I did the "Get Fit, Firm and Pain Free!" workout *(p. 118)*

HOW I FEEL TODAY *(0 = very bad, 10 = very good)*

Pain Scale _____, Mobility/physical ability scale_____

OTHER COMMENTS *(Strategies that worked, inflammation triggers, medication notes or reminders, doctors' appointments, etc.)*

_____
_____
_____
_____
_____

DAY
13

eat right!
Wholegrains demystified

Before buying what you think is a wholegrain product, check the ingredients list, and apply the rules below.

Wheat: If you don't see the word "whole," it is made from refined wheat flour.

Oats: Whether you see the word "whole" or not, it is made from whole oats.

Rye: You must see the word "whole." Most so-called rye and pumpernickel breads are mainly refined wheat flour.

Corn: Look for the word "whole."

Rice: You must see the word "brown." Brown basmati rice is wholegrain; basmati rice is refined.

keep moving!
A cool move in the pool

Zigzags: Get a cardio blast, and work your abs, obliques, and back muscles with I- to 5-minute intervals of zigzag running, resting as needed. Run in a zigzag pattern across the pool, using your arms and legs to push you forward. Keep your chest high, and try not to bend forward as you run.

feel great!
Try an alternative

Guggul supplements, a resin extracted from an Indian desert-dwelling tree, have been shown to have powerful anti-arthritic and anti-inflammatory effects. The recommended dose is 500 mg of standardized guggul extract (standardized to guggul lipids), taken twice daily.

CHECKLIST
(See p62 for your strong-joints eating plan.)

FOOD

Water (8 or more servings)
☐ ☐ ☐ ☐ ☐ ☐ ☐ ☐

Vegetables (3 or more servings)
☐ ☐ ☐

Fruits (3 or more servings)
☐ ☐ ☐

Grains (4 to 9 servings)
(at least half from wholegrains)
☐ ☐ ☐ ☐ ☐ ☐ ☐ ☐ ☐

Fish, soya, nuts & legumes
(1 or more servings) ☐

Milk, yoghurt & cheese
(2 or 3 servings) ☐ ☐ ☐

Meat, poultry & eggs
(2 or less servings) ☐ ☐

SUPPLEMENTS

Multivitamin/mineral ☐
with 100% of RNI for most nutrients

Vitamin D: 10 mcg ☐
(only recommended if you are over 65. Try not to exceed 25 mcg per day as high levels reaching 50 mcg can be dangerous)

Vitamin E:
Discuss dosage with your doctor ☐

ACTIVITY DIARY

☐ I walked ___ minutes, ___ miles, or ___ steps *(p. 106)*

☐ I did the "Get Fit, Firm and Pain Free!" workout *(p. 118)*

HOW I FEEL TODAY *(0 = very bad, 10 = very good)*

Pain Scale _____, Mobility/physical ability scale_____

OTHER COMMENTS *(Strategies that worked, inflammation triggers, medication notes or reminders, doctors' appointments, etc.)*

_____
_____
_____
_____

DAY 14

eat right!
Feast like an Eskimo

Sardines fished from the icy waters of northern Quebec provide the local Inuit people with a whopping 2 g of anti-inflammatory omega-3 fats a day. For 2 g of omega-3s, try one helping of sardines—in a salad, with pasta, or right from the can. Choose from sardines in oil, tomato sauce, or brine (the lower calorie option).

keep moving!
No more excuses!

Don't like exercising? Then do a cool-down. Finishing your exercise session with 5 minutes of easy activity can make it more enjoyable. People's last impression of exercise is the one that lingers. With a cool-down, you leave feeling the exercise was easier, so you're more likely to do it again.

feel great!
Relax away pain

Here's a super-simple technique to help you relax and provide some much-needed pain relief. Lie on your back on an exercise mat, blanket, or rug. Bend your knees so that your feet are flat on the floor, hip-width apart and about 12 inches away from your hips (as shown). Keep your shoulders on the floor but elevate your head slightly with a firm pillow or a couple of books. Rest your hands on your ribs, with your elbows out to the sides.

CHECKLIST

(See p62 for your strong-joints eating plan.)

FOOD

Water (8 or more servings)
☐☐☐☐☐☐☐☐

Vegetables (3 or more servings)
☐☐☐

Fruits (3 or more servings)
☐☐☐

Grains (4 to 9 servings)
(at least half from wholegrains)
☐☐☐☐☐☐☐☐☐

Fish, soya, nuts & legumes
(1 or more servings) ☐

Milk, yoghurt & cheese
(2 or 3 servings) ☐☐☐

Meat, poultry & eggs
(2 or less servings) ☐☐

SUPPLEMENTS

Multivitamin/mineral ☐
with 100% of RNI for most nutrients

Vitamin D: 10 mcg ☐
(only recommended if you are over 65. Try not to exceed 25 mcg per day as high levels reaching 50 mcg can be dangerous)

Vitamin E:
Discuss dosage with your doctor ☐

ACTIVITY DIARY

☐ I walked ___ minutes, ___ miles, or ___ steps *(p. 106)*

☐ I did the "Get Fit, Firm and Pain Free!" workout *(p. 118)*

HOW I FEEL TODAY *(0 = very bad, 10 = very good)*

Pain Scale ____, Mobility/physical ability scale____

OTHER COMMENTS *(Strategies that worked, inflammation triggers, medication notes or reminders, doctors' appointments, etc.)*

_____
_____
_____
_____
_____

DAY 15

eat right!
A one-touch chopper

The Electric Mini Chopper from Lakeland provides relief from chopping by hand. Simple to operate with a soft-touch top, the dishwasher-safe chopper is strong enough to chop nuts and sharp enough to chop onions. Available from Lakeland stores around the country, or online at **www.lakelandlimited.co.uk**.

keep moving!
A healthy hip move

Single-Legged Balance:
Standing on one leg, bend into a quarter squat. The goal is to balance on one leg, but use a wall for support if needed. Don't let your knee go past your toes. Hold for 60 seconds (or as long as you can to start, working up to 60 seconds). Repeat three times, then switch legs.

feel great!
Let your chi flow

In Traditional Chinese Medicine, if you increase the flow of chi in the spine, you can ease arthritis pain. To do this, roll a hand towel lengthwise into a tube (long enough to extend the length of your spine). Lie on a bed with the towel underneath your back on the right side of your spine. Breathe deeply and press underneath the knuckle below the little finger on your right hand; press up towards the knuckle and at a slight angle towards your fourth (ring) finger. Hold the pressure for four or five breaths.

CHECKLIST

(See p62 for your strong-joints eating plan.)

FOOD

Water (8 or more servings)
☐ ☐ ☐ ☐ ☐ ☐ ☐ ☐

Vegetables (3 or more servings)
☐ ☐ ☐

Fruits (3 or more servings)
☐ ☐ ☐

Grains (4 to 9 servings)
(at least half from wholegrains)
☐ ☐ ☐ ☐ ☐ ☐ ☐ ☐ ☐

Fish, soya, nuts & legumes
(1 or more servings) ☐

Milk, yoghurt & cheese
(2 or 3 servings) ☐ ☐ ☐

Meat, poultry & eggs
(2 or less servings) ☐ ☐

SUPPLEMENTS

Multivitamin/mineral ☐
with 100% of RNI for most nutrients

Vitamin D: 10 mcg ☐
(only recommended if you are over 65. Try not to exceed 25 mcg per day as high levels reaching 50 mcg can be dangerous)

Vitamin E:
Discuss dosage with your doctor ☐

ACTIVITY DIARY

☐ I walked ____ minutes, ____ miles, or ____ steps *(p. 106)*

☐ I did the "Get Fit, Firm and Pain Free!" workout *(p. 118)*

HOW I FEEL TODAY *(0 = very bad, 10 = very good)*

Pain Scale _____, Mobility/physical ability scale_____

OTHER COMMENTS *(Strategies that worked, inflammation triggers, medication notes or reminders, doctors' appointments, etc.)*

_____

_____

_____

_____

eat right!
Fishy business

For an omega-3–rich switch, use skinless, boneless salmon to replace the tuna in tuna salad: mix I portion of salmon (7.I oz) with 50 g of reduced-fat mayonnaise, 250 g of chopped cucumber, 75 g of chopped onion, and ¼ teaspoon of dried dillweed. Makes 500 g. **Per 125 g serving:** 105 kcal, 4 g fat, 458 mg sodium, I g fibre

keep moving!
Make your feet happy

If you suffer foot pain, orthotics can provide extra cush-ioning and take pressure off sore spots. Try these tips.

▶ **Support your sport.** When you start an exercise programme, some pain in the ball or heel of the foot is common. Try an insert that provides increased cushioning such as Dr Scholl's Advantage Sport.

▶ **Give it a week.** If your feet still hurt, see your doctor.

▶ **Pad dress shoes.** Dress shoe orthotics can relieve foot pain and fatigue. Try Airplus, Dr Scholl's, or ProFoot.

feel great!
Get a support network

Get to know other people with arthritis so you can share advice and concerns. Knowing that there is someone else who is going through the same thing can be a great comfort. Call **Arthritis Care** for free on **0808 800 4050** to find out where your local support group meet. Or visit **www.rheumatoid.org** and join the members' forum for online support and discussion.

CHECKLIST

(See p62 for your strong-joints eating plan.)

FOOD

Water (8 or more servings)
☐ ☐ ☐ ☐ ☐ ☐ ☐ ☐

Vegetables (3 or more servings)
☐ ☐ ☐

Fruits (3 or more servings)
☐ ☐ ☐

Grains (4 to 9 servings)
(at least half from wholegrains)
☐ ☐ ☐ ☐ ☐ ☐ ☐ ☐ ☐

Fish, soya, nuts & legumes
(1 or more servings) ☐

Milk, yoghurt & cheese
(2 or 3 servings) ☐ ☐ ☐

Meat, poultry & eggs
(2 or less servings) ☐ ☐

SUPPLEMENTS

Multivitamin/mineral ☐
with 100% of RNI for most nutrients

Vitamin D: 10 mcg ☐
(only recommended if you are over 65. Try not to exceed 25 mcg per day as high levels reaching 50 mcg can be dangerous)

Vitamin E:
Discuss dosage with your doctor ☐

ACTIVITY DIARY

☐ I walked ___ minutes, ___ miles, or ___ steps *(p. 106)*

☐ I did the "Get Fit, Firm and Pain Free!" workout *(p. 118)*

HOW I FEEL TODAY *(0 = very bad, 10 = very good)*

Pain Scale _____, Mobility/physical ability scale_____

OTHER COMMENTS *(Strategies that worked, inflammation triggers, medication notes or reminders, doctors' appointments, etc.)*

_____
_____
_____
_____
_____

DAY 17

eat right!
Naturally sweet

Try natural sweeteners as an alternative to highly refined white sugar—sprinkle chopped, dried fruit on top of your cereal, or stir a spoon of honey into your porridge or hot drink. And if possible, learn to love the taste of tea itself, so you don't need to disguise it with any sweetener at all.

keep moving!
Think "yes, I can!"

Generating positive thoughts can help you exercise better. It may feel artificial at first, but research shows that people who use positive self-talk, actually saying to themselves, "I'm strong; I'm able; I can do this," really do perform better than those who talk negatively.

feel great!
Take a nap

Sleep restores your energy so that you can better manage pain. It also rests joints to reduce pain and swelling. If you feel tired and achy after lunch, take a brief nap (15 to 20 minutes). If you have trouble sleeping at night, try relaxing quietly in the afternoon rather than taking a nap.

CHECKLIST
(See p62 for your strong-joints eating plan.)

FOOD

Water (8 or more servings)
☐ ☐ ☐ ☐ ☐ ☐ ☐ ☐

Vegetables (3 or more servings)
☐ ☐ ☐

Fruits (3 or more servings)
☐ ☐ ☐

Grains (4 to 9 servings)
(at least half from wholegrains)
☐ ☐ ☐ ☐ ☐ ☐ ☐ ☐ ☐

Fish, soya, nuts & legumes
(1 or more servings) ☐

Milk, yoghurt & cheese
(2 or 3 servings) ☐ ☐ ☐

Meat, poultry & eggs
(2 or less servings) ☐ ☐

SUPPLEMENTS

Multivitamin/mineral ☐
with 100% of RNI for most nutrients

Vitamin D: 10 mcg ☐
(only recommended if you are over 65. Try not to exceed 25 mcg per day as high levels reaching 50 mcg can be dangerous)

Vitamin E:
Discuss dosage with your doctor ☐

ACTIVITY DIARY

☐ I walked ___ minutes, ___ miles, or ___ steps *(p. 106)*

☐ I did the "Get Fit, Firm and Pain Free!" workout *(p. 118)*

HOW I FEEL TODAY *(0 = very bad, 10 = very good)*

Pain Scale _____, Mobility/physical ability scale_____

OTHER COMMENTS *(Strategies that worked, inflammation triggers, medication notes or reminders, doctors' appointments, etc.)*

_____
_____
_____
_____
_____

DAY 18

eat right!
Easy ways to enjoy berries

▶ Add fresh or thawed frozen berries to your breakfast cereal.

▶ In a container, add a touch of sugar to frozen berries. By lunchtime, they're thawed and delicious.

▶ Serve whole strawberries with a chocolate-syrup dipping sauce for a stylish dessert.

▶ Top spinach salad with 150 g of strawberries. Toss with vinaigrette dressing, and sprinkle with low-fat feta cheese.

▶ For a snack, top a bowl of berries with skimmed milk.

keep moving!
Get noticed

Research clearly shows that you can be seen much more easily when you wear clothing made from reflective material. Nathan's athletic wear has reflective silver beading in the fabric, so the majority of the garment is visible. Products are available from **www.1000mile.co.uk**, or at sports equipment shops nationwide.

feel great!
Rub in some relief

Even if you don't like the hot taste of capsicums —strong peppers and chillies—using liniments or creams made from an extract of the plant is a natural, effective way to relieve pain. It may feel a little warm when you first use it, so be sure to start off with a test patch on a small area of skin.

CHECKLIST

(See p62 for your strong-joints eating plan.)

FOOD

Water (8 or more servings)
☐ ☐ ☐ ☐ ☐ ☐ ☐ ☐

Vegetables (3 or more servings)
☐ ☐ ☐

Fruits (3 or more servings)
☐ ☐ ☐

Grains (4 to 9 servings)
(at least half from wholegrains)
☐ ☐ ☐ ☐ ☐ ☐ ☐ ☐ ☐

Fish, soya, nuts & legumes
(1 or more servings) ☐

Milk, yoghurt & cheese
(2 or 3 servings) ☐ ☐ ☐

Meat, poultry & eggs
(2 or less servings) ☐ ☐

SUPPLEMENTS

Multivitamin/mineral ☐
with 100% of RNI for most nutrients

Vitamin D: 10 mcg ☐
(only recommended if you are over 65. Try not to exceed 25 mcg per day as high levels reaching 50 mcg can be dangerous)

Vitamin E:
Discuss dosage with your doctor ☐

ACTIVITY DIARY

☐ I walked ___ minutes, ___ miles, or ___ steps *(p. 106)*

☐ I did the "Get Fit, Firm and Pain Free!" workout *(p. 118)*

HOW I FEEL TODAY *(0 = very bad, 10 = very good)*

Pain Scale ____, Mobility/physical ability scale____

OTHER COMMENTS *(Strategies that worked, inflammation triggers, medication notes or reminders, doctors' appointments, etc.)*

_____

_____

_____

_____

DAY 19

eat right!
Easy top-popper
No need to struggle opening stubborn jars, or risk chipping the glass by banging lids on counters. There are lots of gadgets to make it easier, but one of the simplest—and cheapest—is the Jar Gripper. Or for brand new jars, a Jar Key breaks the vacuum and prises the lid off with no problems. Both are available from Lakeland Limited at **www.lakelandlimited.co.uk**. Call **015394 88100** to find your nearest store.

keep moving!
Get a fragrant boost
Dragging in the gym? Dab some peppermint oil on your collar. In a study at America's Wheeling Jesuit University in West Virginia, 40 athletes ran faster and did more press-ups when exposed to peppermint scent than with other or no scents. Peppermint boosts mood, so you perform better without working harder.

feel great!
Acupressure
To relieve pain in your feet, try the GB41 acupressure point, found on top of your foot between your fourth and fifth toes. Starting at the web between your toes, slide your fingers between the bones towards your ankle. You'll find a notch where those bones meet; the point is in that notch and will usually be quite sensitive. Press for 1 to 2 minutes.

CHECKLIST
(See p62 for your strong-joints eating plan.)

FOOD

Water (8 or more servings)
☐ ☐ ☐ ☐ ☐ ☐ ☐ ☐

Vegetables (3 or more servings)
☐ ☐ ☐

Fruits (3 or more servings)
☐ ☐ ☐

Grains (4 to 9 servings)
(at least half from wholegrains)
☐ ☐ ☐ ☐ ☐ ☐ ☐ ☐ ☐

Fish, soya, nuts & legumes
(1 or more servings)
☐

Milk, yoghurt & cheese
(2 or 3 servings)
☐ ☐ ☐

Meat, poultry & eggs
(2 or less servings)
☐ ☐

SUPPLEMENTS

Multivitamin/mineral
with 100% of RNI for most nutrients
☐

Vitamin D: 10 mcg
(only recommended if you are over 65. Try not to exceed 25 mcg per day as high levels reaching 50 mcg can be dangerous)

Vitamin E: Discuss dosage with your doctor
☐

ACTIVITY DIARY

☐ I walked ___ minutes, ___ miles, or ___ steps *(p. 106)*

☐ I did the "Get Fit, Firm and Pain Free!" workout *(p. 118)*

HOW I FEEL TODAY *(0 = very bad, 10 = very good)*

Pain Scale ____, Mobility/physical ability scale____

OTHER COMMENTS *(Strategies that worked, inflammation triggers, medication notes or reminders, doctors' appointments, etc.)*

_____
_____
_____
_____
_____

DAY 20

eat right!
Diet monitoring

There are lots of methods of allergy-testing that claim to be able to detect foods that might trigger your arthritis, but none of them are proven to work. The only sure-fire way to decide if any particular food stuffs worsen your condition is to exclude them —one at a time—from your diet and keep a careful, written record of your health. But don't embark on an exclusion diet without talking to your doctor first.

keep moving!
Exclusive swimming

If you feel uncomfortable about going swimming when the pool is crowded, find a local pool that has time set aside for women-only (or men-only) adult swimming. Most pools will have one evening a week for this, and will do their best to make sure that the lifeguards on duty are all women, too. In the summer, if you are feeling brave, venture to an outdoor pool, so that you can get a vitamin D boost from the sun while you exercise.

feel great!
Let yourself go

On holiday, that is. To relieve stress and pain, take a trip. Make yours a good one by remembering to bring extra medication, a spare prescription, insurance documents, comfortable shoes, and your doctor's contact details. The website **www.arthritiscarehotels.org.uk** features four hotels that cater specifically for people with arthritis and their carers.

CHECKLIST
(See p62 for your strong-joints eating plan.)

FOOD

Water (8 or more servings)
☐☐☐☐☐☐☐☐

Vegetables (3 or more servings)
☐☐☐

Fruits (3 or more servings)
☐☐☐

Grains (4 to 9 servings)
(at least half from wholegrains)
☐☐☐☐☐☐☐☐☐

Fish, soya, nuts & legumes
(1 or more servings) ☐

Milk, yoghurt & cheese
(2 or 3 servings) ☐☐☐

Meat, poultry & eggs
(2 or less servings) ☐☐

SUPPLEMENTS

Multivitamin/mineral ☐
with 100% of RNI for most nutrients

Vitamin D: 10 mcg ☐
(only recommended if you are over 65. Try not to exceed 25 mcg per day as high levels reaching 50 mcg can be dangerous)

Vitamin E:
Discuss dosage with your doctor ☐

ACTIVITY DIARY

☐ I walked ___ minutes, ___ miles, or ___ steps *(p. 106)*

☐ I did the "Get Fit, Firm and Pain Free!" workout *(p. 118)*

HOW I FEEL TODAY *(0 = very bad, 10 = very good)*

Pain Scale ____, Mobility/physical ability scale____

OTHER COMMENTS *(Strategies that worked, inflammation triggers, medication notes or reminders, doctors' appointments, etc.)*

_____
_____
_____
_____
_____

DAY 21

eat right!
Eat to sleep

Sleep is a precious commodity for people with arthritis. Avoid sleep-busters such as caffeine and alcohol for at least 5 hours before going to bed. For a sleep-promoting bedtime snack, try a high-carb bowl of wholegrain cereal sprinkled with fruit, or a bowl of warm oatmeal.

keep moving!
Treat your feet

A foot spa is the perfect way to pamper yourself after a long day on your feet. Hydrotherapy can help reduce soreness and swelling. The warm circulating water acts like a mini-massage to relieve tension and rejuvenate tired muscles. Foot spas are available at department and larger chemist stores. Prices range from £45 to £100. Note: If you have diabetes or poor circulation, check with your doctor first.

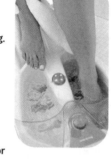

feel great!
Are you sitting comfortably?

Sitting comfortably is essential, so make sure that using your favourite chair isn't aggravating your arthritis. It should be high enough that your bare feet are flat on the floor when you sit in it, with firm, padded armrests around 9 inches above the seat of the chair, so you don't hunch when you use them. Chairs with wooden-ended armrests and room beneath them at the front are easier to get out of.

CHECKLIST
(See p62 for your strong-joints eating plan.)

FOOD

Water (8 or more servings)
☐ ☐ ☐ ☐ ☐ ☐ ☐ ☐

Vegetables (3 or more servings)
☐ ☐ ☐

Fruits (3 or more servings)
☐ ☐ ☐

Grains (4 to 9 servings)
(at least half from wholegrains)
☐ ☐ ☐ ☐ ☐ ☐ ☐ ☐ ☐

Fish, soya, nuts & legumes
(1 or more servings) ☐

Milk, yoghurt & cheese
(2 or 3 servings) ☐ ☐ ☐

Meat, poultry & eggs
(2 or less servings) ☐ ☐

SUPPLEMENTS

Multivitamin/mineral ☐
with 100% of RNI for most nutrients

Vitamin D: 10 mcg ☐
(only recommended if you are over 65. Try not to exceed 25 mcg per day as high levels reaching 50 mcg can be dangerous)

Vitamin E:
Discuss dosage with your doctor ☐

ACTIVITY DIARY

☐ I walked ____ minutes, ____ miles, or ____ steps *(p. 106)*

☐ I did the "Get Fit, Firm and Pain Free!" workout *(p. 118)*

HOW I FEEL TODAY *(0 = very bad, 10 = very good)*

Pain Scale ____, Mobility/physical ability scale____

OTHER COMMENTS *(Strategies that worked, inflammation triggers, medication notes or reminders, doctors' appointments, etc.)*

_____

_____

_____

_____

_____

DAY 22

eat right!
See the light

If you are trying to lose weight or reduce your fat intake, be wary of any labels on food that declares it is "Lite" or "Light." As the Food Standards Agency has no official definition of these terms, these foods might not contain any fewer grams of fat or calories than the standard equivalent. Look out for "low-fat," which must be 3 g of fat per 100 g. And remember, anything that is "80% fat-free" contains 20 g of fat per 100 g, which is certainly not a low level.

keep moving!
Rise to the challenge

This easy move will strengthen your walking muscles.
Double Toe Raise (works feet and shins): Sit in a chair with your feet flat on the floor. Lift just your toes, then lift the rest of your foot, with your heels staying on the floor. Lower your foot, then your toes. Repeat 8 to 12 times. Do two or three times a week.

feel great!
Be aware of your options

In the past 2 years, the National Institute for Clinical Excellence has approved several drugs for rheumatoid arthritis, osteoarthritis, and other arthritis-related diseases. If your current medication isn't working as well as you'd like—or if it's causing unacceptable side effects—ask your doctor about these new treatment options.

CHECKLIST

(See p62 for your strong-joints eating plan.)

FOOD

Water (8 or more servings)
☐ ☐ ☐ ☐ ☐ ☐ ☐ ☐

Vegetables (3 or more servings)
☐ ☐ ☐

Fruits (3 or more servings)
☐ ☐ ☐

Grains (4 to 9 servings)
(at least half from wholegrains)
☐ ☐ ☐ ☐ ☐ ☐ ☐ ☐

Fish, soya, nuts & legumes
(1 or more servings) ☐

Milk, yoghurt & cheese
(2 or 3 servings) ☐ ☐ ☐

Meat, poultry & eggs
(2 or less servings) ☐ ☐

SUPPLEMENTS

Multivitamin/mineral
with 100% of RNI for most nutrients ☐

Vitamin D: 10 mcg ☐
(only recommended if you are over 65. Try not to exceed 25 mcg per day as high levels reaching 50 mcg can be dangerous)

Vitamin E:
Discuss dosage with your doctor ☐

ACTIVITY DIARY

☐ I walked ___ minutes, ___ miles, or ___ steps *(p. 106)*

☐ I did the "Get Fit, Firm and Pain Free!" workout *(p. 118)*

HOW I FEEL TODAY *(0 = very bad, 10 = very good)*

Pain Scale ___, Mobility/physical ability scale ___

OTHER COMMENTS *(Strategies that worked, inflammation triggers, medication notes or reminders, doctors' appointments, etc.)*

_____
_____
_____
_____
_____

DAY 23

eat right!
More cool water tricks

To get your 8 or more glasses of water a day, add just a few ice cubes to your water bottle or glass, or try it ice-free. You'll be able to drink more water if it's cool or room temperature rather than icy cold. And thirsty or not, have a glass between meals.

keep moving!
A kinder, gentler workout

Tai chi is an ancient Chinese practice performed to improve the flow of energy in the body. The slow, gentle, deliberate moves are based on animal movements, done continuously, all while standing. It improves balance, stamina, and coordination, and studies show it helps reduce arthritis pain. Visit the **Tai Chi Union** at www.taichiunion.com, or call **0141 810 3482** to find your nearest class.

feel great!
Know your rights

Know your rights, and don't be intimidated by the medical professionals. The *Guide to the NHS* states that you can choose whether you take part in research. When you go to an outpatient clinic, you should have to wait a maximum of 30 minutes for your appointment. Staff must respect your privacy and dignity, and not discriminate against you on the basis of sex, age, religion, or sexuality. For a copy of the guide call **0800 555 777**.

CHECKLIST
(See p62 for your strong-joints eating plan.)

FOOD

Water (8 or more servings)
☐☐☐☐☐☐☐☐

Vegetables (3 or more servings)
☐☐☐

Fruits (3 or more servings)
☐☐☐

Grains (4 to 9 servings)
(at least half from wholegrains)
☐☐☐☐☐☐☐☐☐

Fish, soya, nuts & legumes
(1 or more servings) ☐

Milk, yoghurt & cheese
(2 or 3 servings) ☐☐☐

Meat, poultry & eggs
(2 or less servings) ☐☐

SUPPLEMENTS

Multivitamin/mineral ☐
with 100% of RNI for most nutrients

Vitamin D: 10 mcg ☐
(only recommended if you are over 65. Try not to exceed 25 mcg per day as high levels reaching 50 mcg can be dangerous)

Vitamin E:
Discuss dosage with your doctor ☐

ACTIVITY DIARY

☐ I walked ___ minutes, ___ miles, or ___ steps *(p. 106)*

☐ I did the "Get Fit, Firm and Pain Free!" workout *(p. 118)*

HOW I FEEL TODAY *(0 = very bad, 10 = very good)*

Pain Scale ___, Mobility/physical ability scale___

OTHER COMMENTS *(Strategies that worked, inflammation triggers, medication notes or reminders, doctors' appointments, etc.)*

_____
_____
_____
_____
_____

DAY 24

eat right!
Mackerel to start

Mackerel is rich in omega-3 fatty acids, but it can be too rich to eat as a main course. Why not try this easy-to-prepare pâté as a starter? Blend smoked mackerel fillets with fromage frais (or natural yoghurt) and fresh chives until smooth. Then add salt, pepper and lemon juice to taste. Serve with crisp, wholewheat toast and a wedge of lemon.

keep moving!
Get the scale moving

You walk an hour a day, 7 days a week, but the weight won't budge. Here's how to jump-start your weight loss.
Go harder, not longer. Trekking up hills or doing speed-interval sessions boosts the intensity of your workout.
Surprise your body. Cross-training is a great way to blast off a plateau. Replace a couple of walks a week with cycling or swimming.
Pick up a dumbbell. The more muscle you have, the more calories you burn—without even trying. Lift weights that are heavy enough to fatigue your muscles.

feel great!
Needle away pain

Evidence suggests that acupuncture can help restore health to people with arthritis. It can be especially helpful in alleviating chronic pain and fatigue. Choose a practitioner certified by the **British Medical Acupuncture Society** on **020 7387 9642**.

CHECKLIST
(See p62 for your strong-joints eating plan.)

FOOD

Water (8 or more servings)
☐ ☐ ☐ ☐ ☐ ☐ ☐ ☐

Vegetables (3 or more servings)
☐ ☐ ☐

Fruits (3 or more servings)
☐ ☐ ☐

Grains (4 to 9 servings)
(at least half from wholegrains)
☐ ☐ ☐ ☐ ☐ ☐ ☐ ☐ ☐

Fish, soya, nuts & legumes
(1 or more servings) ☐

Milk, yoghurt & cheese
(2 or 3 servings) ☐ ☐ ☐

Meat, poultry & eggs
(2 or less servings) ☐ ☐

SUPPLEMENTS

Multivitamin/mineral ☐
with 100% of RNI for most nutrients

Vitamin D: 10 mcg ☐
(only recommended if you are over 65. Try not to exceed 25 mcg per day as high levels reaching 50 mcg can be dangerous)

Vitamin E:
Discuss dosage with your doctor ☐

ACTIVITY DIARY

☐ I walked ____ minutes, ____ miles, or ____ steps *(p. 106)*

☐ I did the "Get Fit, Firm and Pain Free!" workout *(p. 118)*

HOW I FEEL TODAY *(0 = very bad, 10 = very good)*

Pain Scale _____, Mobility/physical ability scale_____

OTHER COMMENTS *(Strategies that worked, inflammation triggers, medication notes or reminders, doctors' appointments, etc.)*

_____
_____
_____
_____
_____

DAY 25

eat right!
What not to eat

If you have RA, avoid meats and foods high in saturated fat. Avoid processed foods. Some people are sensitive to wheat, gluten, dairy foods, corn, citrus fruits, tomatoes, and eggs—these foods can switch on the body's inflammatory response. Also avoid refined sugar, salt, alcohol, and caffeine.

keep moving!
Instant aah!

Stretching your hips will increase your range of motion and reduce your risk of injury. Here's a quick stretch you can do after a few minutes of warm-up walking:

I. Find a high curb or step to stand on and something to hold for balance. (You can use a step and railing indoors.)

2. Stand with your feet parallel to the curb, one foot on the curb and the other hanging free.

3. Lower the hanging leg by dropping your hip. Keep both knees straight. This stretches the hip of the leg on the curb. Hold for 15 to 60 seconds. Repeat on the other side.

feel great!
The write stuff

If your fingers are stiff, writing can be difficult. Using ergonomically designed pens and pencils makes it less painful—check out the Dr Grip range at **www.pilotpen.co.uk**, or **www.bicmarker.com**. Or you can fit rubber grips to your ordinary pens and pencils. The Weston Health online catalogue at **www.westons.com** has a range of products to make writing easier.

CHECKLIST

(See p62 for your strong-joints eating plan.)

FOOD

Water (8 or more servings)
☐ ☐ ☐ ☐ ☐ ☐ ☐ ☐

Vegetables (3 or more servings)
☐ ☐ ☐

Fruits (3 or more servings)
☐ ☐ ☐

Grains (4 to 9 servings)
(at least half from wholegrains)
☐ ☐ ☐ ☐ ☐ ☐ ☐ ☐ ☐

Fish, soya, nuts & legumes
(1 or more servings) ☐

Milk, yoghurt & cheese
(2 or 3 servings) ☐ ☐ ☐

Meat, poultry & eggs
(2 or less servings) ☐ ☐

SUPPLEMENTS

Multivitamin/mineral ☐
with 100% of RNI for most nutrients

Vitamin D: 10 mcg ☐
(only recommended if you are over 65. Try not to exceed 25 mcg per day as high levels reaching 50 mcg can be dangerous)

Vitamin E:
Discuss dosage with your doctor ☐

ACTIVITY DIARY

☐ I walked ___ minutes, ___ miles, or ___ steps *(p. 106)*

☐ I did the "Get Fit, Firm and Pain Free!" workout *(p. 118)*

HOW I FEEL TODAY *(0 = very bad, 10 = very good)*

Pain Scale ___, Mobility/physical ability scale___

OTHER COMMENTS *(Strategies that worked, inflammation triggers, medication notes or reminders, doctors' appointments, etc.)*

_____

_____

_____

_____

_____

DAY 26

eat right!
Healthy baking

Alter your favourite baking recipes by subsituting a quarter of the butter, margarine, or oil with ground flaxseed, for a tasty omega-3 boost. Use three table-spoons of seed for every one of conventional fat. You can grind flaxseeds using a coffee grinder, and remember that your baking will brown a little quicker using this subsitution, so keep an eye on the oven while it's cooking.

keep moving!
Fast back relief

This simple move eases back pain: lie back on a firm Styrofoam cylinder extended along your spine from your bottom to your neck with your feet flat on the floor. Raise your arms straight up so your hands point up towards the ceiling. Lift your right foot off the floor. Slowly move your arms to the right until they are almost parallel to the floor. Then move to the other side. Bring your arms back to centre. Then switch legs, and repeat; continue switching sides for 10 minutes. Do this move once or twice daily.

feel great!
Play in the dirt

Digging in the dirt can be therapeutic for sore hands and can yield beautiful and fragrant—or delicious and nutritious—results. Choose low-maintenance plants, such as shrubs or herbacious perennials, and fill easy-to-reach containers with annuals on the patio near the house.

CHECKLIST

(See p62 for your strong-joints eating plan.)

FOOD

Water (8 or more servings)
☐☐☐☐☐☐☐☐

Vegetables (3 or more servings)
☐☐☐

Fruits (3 or more servings)
☐☐☐

Grains (4 to 9 servings)
(at least half from wholegrains)
☐☐☐☐☐☐☐☐☐

Fish, soya, nuts & legumes
(1 or more servings) ☐

Milk, yoghurt & cheese
(2 or 3 servings) ☐☐☐

Meat, poultry & eggs
(2 or less servings) ☐☐

SUPPLEMENTS

Multivitamin/mineral ☐
with 100% of RNI for most nutrients

Vitamin D: 10 mcg ☐
(only recommended if you are over 65. Try not to exceed 25 mcg per day as high levels reaching 50 mcg can be dangerous)

Vitamin E:
Discuss dosage with your doctor ☐

ACTIVITY DIARY

☐ I walked ___ minutes, ___ miles, or ___ steps *(p. 106)*

☐ I did the "Get Fit, Firm and Pain Free!" workout *(p. 118)*

HOW I FEEL TODAY *(0 = very bad, 10 = very good)*

Pain Scale ___, Mobility/physical ability scale___

OTHER COMMENTS *(Strategies that worked, inflammation triggers, medication notes or reminders, doctors' appointments, etc.)*

_____

_____

_____

_____

_____

eat right!
Don't make this microwave mistake

Many people come home from work and pop a frozen starter into the microwave. But eating too many processed foods can leave you short on fibre and antioxidants such as vitamin C. The smarter choice is to complement a frozen starter with a green salad, a 100% wholewheat roll, and a fruit for dessert.

keep moving!
Get into a great book

Tune in to an audio book while you walk. It'll keep you going longer and looking forward to the next walk—and the next chapter! Check your local library for a great selection. Look for a whodunnit; you might walk so far you'll need to take a cab home! *NB:* Make sure you can still hear surrounding sounds.

feel great!
Slow arthritis damage

In a Belgian study following 212 people with osteoarthritis of the knee for 3 years, the supplement glucosamine not only relieved their pain but also slowed destruction of the protective cartilage lining their knee joints. Glucosamine may take anywhere from 2 weeks to 2 months to provide pain relief. Before you start taking any supplements, check with your doctor to make certain they won't interfere with any medication you may be on.

CHECKLIST
(See p62 for your strong-joints eating plan.)

FOOD

Water (8 or more servings)
☐ ☐ ☐ ☐ ☐ ☐ ☐ ☐

Vegetables (3 or more servings)
☐ ☐ ☐

Fruits (3 or more servings)
☐ ☐ ☐

Grains (4 to 9 servings)
(at least half from wholegrains)
☐ ☐ ☐ ☐ ☐ ☐ ☐ ☐ ☐

Fish, soya, nuts & legumes
(1 or more servings) ☐

Milk, yoghurt & cheese
(2 or 3 servings) ☐ ☐ ☐

Meat, poultry & eggs
(2 or less servings) ☐ ☐

SUPPLEMENTS

Multivitamin/mineral ☐
with 100% of RNI for most nutrients

Vitamin D: 10 mcg ☐
(only recommended if you are over 65. Try not to exceed 25 mcg per day as high levels reaching 50 mcg can be dangerous)

Vitamin E:
Discuss dosage with your doctor ☐

ACTIVITY DIARY

☐ I walked ___ minutes, ___ miles, or ___ steps *(p. 106)*

☐ I did the "Get Fit, Firm and Pain Free!" workout *(p. 118)*

HOW I FEEL TODAY *(0 = very bad, 10 = very good)*

Pain Scale ___, Mobility/physical ability scale___

OTHER COMMENTS *(Strategies that worked, inflammation triggers, medication notes or reminders, doctors' appointments, etc.)*

_____

_____

_____

_____

DAY 28

eat right!
Keep the water flowing

Try some more easy tricks to get 8 or more glasses of water a day:

▶ Keep a glass of water on your bedside table, and drink it all down before you even get out of bed.

▶ Never walk by a water fountain without stopping.

▶ Estimate that 10 big gulps equals 300 ml of water.

▶ Start meals with soup. They're mostly water.

▶ Drink on schedule. Write it on your calendar, or programme the alarm on your watch to beep every hour. Each time you are reminded, drink a glass of water.

keep moving!
Beat a bad mood

Got the blues? Studies have shown that even mild exercise, about 40% of your maximum heart rate, can lift your mood. So, if you're not up for the usual high-energy stuff, do some leisure activity you enjoy, such as digging in your garden or walking in a park.

feel great!
Try the "mushroom of immortality"

The reishi mushroom is a safe and effective natural anti-inflammatory. Look for reishi at your local health food store; follow the dosage instruction on the label. Try it for 2 months to see if it helps ease your pain.

CHECKLIST

(See p62 for your strong-joints eating plan.)

FOOD

Water (8 or more servings)
☐☐☐☐☐☐☐☐

Vegetables (3 or more servings)
☐☐☐

Fruits (3 or more servings)
☐☐☐

Grains (4 to 9 servings)
(at least half from wholegrains)
☐☐☐☐☐☐☐☐☐

Fish, soya, nuts & legumes
(1 or more servings) ☐

Milk, yoghurt & cheese
(2 or 3 servings) ☐☐☐

Meat, poultry & eggs
(2 or less servings) ☐☐

SUPPLEMENTS

Multivitamin/mineral ☐
with 100% of RNI for most nutrients

Vitamin D: 10 mcg ☐
(only recommended if you are over 65. Try not to exceed 25 mcg per day as high levels reaching 50 mcg can be dangerous)

Vitamin E:
Discuss dosage with your doctor ☐

ACTIVITY DIARY

☐ I walked ___ minutes, ___ miles, or ___ steps *(p. 106)*

☐ I did the "Get Fit, Firm and Pain Free!" workout *(p. 118)*

HOW I FEEL TODAY *(0 = very bad, 10 = very good)*

Pain Scale _____, Mobility/physical ability scale_____

OTHER COMMENTS *(Strategies that worked, inflammation triggers, medication notes or reminders, doctors' appointments, etc.)*

_____
_____
_____
_____
_____

DAY 29

eat right!
Liquid nutrition

Three-quarters of a cup of tomato-based vegetable juice (such as V8) has more than twice as much of the powerful antioxidant lycopene as a cup of chopped fresh tomatoes. Add a generous dose of vitamin C and an array of carotenoids donated by the other vegetables in the juice, and you're drinking liquid nutrition.

keep moving!
Burn 60% more calories

Crank up the incline on your treadmill, and increase your calorie burn by up to 60%. Here's how.

Don't lean. Maintain an upright posture; keep your shoulders over your hips, and your hips over your ankles.

Start easy. Do a 5-minute slow walk and then a 10-minute brisk pace before adding your first hill.

Go 5 and 5. Alternate 5-minute hills with 5 minutes of level walking. Repeat as often as you like. Cool down for 5 minutes.

feel great!
Go online

Find the resources you need by contacting one of the national arthritis charities. Contact the **National Rheumatoid Arthritis Society (NRAS)** on **01628 670606, Arthritis Care** on **020 7380 6500** or **Arthritis Research Campaign (ARC)** on **0870 850 5000**. They offer advice and support for arthritis sufferers, and those who care for them.

CHECKLIST

(See p62 for your strong-joints eating plan.)

FOOD

Water (8 or more servings)
☐ ☐ ☐ ☐ ☐ ☐ ☐ ☐

Vegetables (3 or more servings)
☐ ☐ ☐

Fruits (3 or more servings)
☐ ☐ ☐

Grains (4 to 9 servings)
(at least half from wholegrains)
☐ ☐ ☐ ☐ ☐ ☐ ☐ ☐ ☐

Fish, soya, nuts & legumes
(1 or more servings) ☐

Milk, yoghurt & cheese
(2 or 3 servings) ☐ ☐ ☐

Meat, poultry & eggs
(2 or less servings) ☐ ☐

SUPPLEMENTS

Multivitamin/mineral ☐
with 100% of RNI for most nutrients

Vitamin D: 10 mcg ☐
(only recommended if you are over 65. Try not to exceed 25 mcg per day as high levels reaching 50 mcg can be dangerous)

Vitamin E:
Discuss dosage with your doctor ☐

ACTIVITY DIARY

☐ I walked ___ minutes, ___ miles, or ___ steps *(p. 106)*

☐ I did the "Get Fit, Firm and Pain Free!" workout *(p. 118)*

HOW I FEEL TODAY *(0 = very bad, 10 = very good)*

Pain Scale ___, Mobility/physical ability scale___

OTHER COMMENTS *(Strategies that worked, inflammation triggers, medication notes or reminders, doctors' appointments, etc.)*

_____
_____
_____
_____
_____

DAY 30

eat right!
Try Coromega

If you don't like the taste of fish but still want to get the benefits of fish oils, try Coromega, an orange-flavoured supplement that

doesn't have any aftertaste. You can mix it with yoghurt, fruit juice smoothies, or even eat it straight out of the packet. Go to **www.coromega.com** to find out more.

keep moving!
Don't overfuel

Many everyday exercisers chow down on energy bars, sports drinks, and recovery bars that should be reserved for elite athletes. People think they'll supply magical strength, when all they primarily provide is calories. You can easily eat and drink 700 calories for a 200-calorie workout. Stick to a simple piece of fruit, or some nuts and water, if you need a snack.

feel great!
Save your money

The pain and chronic nature of arthritis force some people to try almost anything for relief, even unproven or downright harmful remedies. When in doubt, ask your doctor. But here are a few products that have been proven not to relieve arthritis.

▶ **Copper bracelets**
▶ **Shark cartilage**
▶ **Alfalfa**
▶ **DMSO (dimethyl sulfoxide)**

CHECKLIST

(See p62 for your strong-joints eating plan.)

FOOD

Water (8 or more servings)
☐ ☐ ☐ ☐ ☐ ☐ ☐ ☐

Vegetables (3 or more servings)
☐ ☐ ☐

Fruits (3 or more servings)
☐ ☐ ☐

Grains (4 to 9 servings)
(at least half from wholegrains)
☐ ☐ ☐ ☐ ☐ ☐ ☐ ☐ ☐

Fish, soya, nuts & legumes
(1 or more servings) ☐

Milk, yoghurt & cheese
(2 or 3 servings) ☐ ☐ ☐

Meat, poultry & eggs
(2 or less servings) ☐ ☐

SUPPLEMENTS

Multivitamin/mineral ☐
with 100% of RNI for most nutrients

Vitamin D: 10 mcg ☐
(only recommended if you are over 65. Try not to exceed 25 mcg per day as high levels reaching 50 mcg can be dangerous)

Vitamin E:
Discuss dosage with your doctor ☐

ACTIVITY DIARY

☐ I walked ___ minutes, ___ miles, or ___ steps *(p. 106)*

☐ I did the "Get Fit, Firm and Pain Free!" workout *(p. 118)*

HOW I FEEL TODAY *(0 = very bad, 10 = very good)*

Pain Scale _____, Mobility/physical ability scale_____

OTHER COMMENTS *(Strategies that worked, inflammation triggers, medication notes or reminders, doctors' appointments, etc.)*

_____
_____
_____
_____
_____

CHAPTER 22

Arthritis Resource

Knowledge is power in the battle against arthritis.
Find all the information you need to know here

Associations and Organisations

ARTHRITIS CARE
18 Stephenson Way
London NW1 2HD
Tel: 020 7380 6500 (General enquiries)
Helpline: 0808 800 4050
Fax: 020 7380 6505
Web: www.arthritiscare.org.uk

ARTHRITIS RESEARCH CAMPAIGN (ARC)
Copeman House
St Mary's Court
St Mary's Gate
Chesterfield
Derbyshire S41 7TD
Tel: 0870 850 5000
or 01246 558033
Fax: 01246 558007
e-mail: Info@arc.org.uk
Web: www.arc.org.uk

CHILDREN'S CHRONIC ARTHRITIS
ASSOCIATION
Ground Floor
Amber Gate
City Wall Road
Worcester, WR1 2AH
Tel: 01905 745595

Fax: 01905 745703
e-mail: info@ccaa.org.uk
Web: www.ccaa.org.uk

DISABILITY ALLIANCE
Universal House
88-94 Wentworth Street
London E1 7SA
Tel: 020 7247 8776
Fax: 020 7247 8765
Web: www.disabilityalliance.org

DISABLED LIVING
CENTRES COUNCIL
Redbank House
4 St Chad's Street
Chetham
Manchester M8 8QA
Tel: 0161 834 1044
Fax: 0161 839 0802
e-mail: dlcc@dlcc.org.uk
Web: www.dlcc.org.uk

DISABLED LIVING
FOUNDATION
380-384 Harrow Road
London W9 2HU
Tel: 020 7289 6111 (General enquiries)
Helpline: 0845 130 9177
Web: www.dlf.org.uk

DEPARTMENT OF WORK AND PENSIONS
Web: www.dwp.gov.uk/lifeevent/
discare/index.asp; www.disability.gov.uk
Tel: 0800 882200

DISABILITY RIGHTS COMMISSION
FREEPOST MID02164
Stratford upon Avon CV37 9BR
Tel: 08457 622 633 **Fax:** 08457 778 878
Web: www.drc.org.uk

EXPERT PATIENTS PROGRAMME
Tel: 0845 6066040
Web: www.expertpatients.nhs.uk

FIBROMYALGIA ASSOCIATION UK
PO Box 206
Stourbridge DY9 8YL
Tel: 0870 220 1232
e-mail: fmauk@hotmail.com
Web: www.fibromyalgia-associationuk.org

LUPUS UK
St James House,
Eastern Road
Romford
Essex RM1 3NH
Tel: 01708 731251
Fax: 01708 731252
e-mail: headoffice@lupus-uk.freeserve.co.uk
Web: www.lupusuk.com

NATIONAL ANKYLOSING SPONDYLITIS
ASSOCATION (NASS)
PO Box 179
Mayfield
East Sussex TN2O 6ZL
Tel: 01435 873527 **Fax:** 01435 873027
e-mail: nass@nass.co.uk
Web: www.nass.co.uk

NATIONAL RHEUMATOID ARTHRITIS
SOCIETY (NRAS)
Briarwood House
11 College Avenue
Maidenhead
Berkshire SL6 6AR
Tel: 01628 670606
Fax: 01628 638810
e-mail: enquiries@rheumatoid.org.uk
Web: www.rheumatoid.org

PAIN CONCERN UK
PO Box 318
Canterbury
Kent CT2 0GD
Tel: 01227 712183
Helpline: 01227 710402
Fax: 01227 713402
e-mail: painconcern@btinternet.com
Web:www.painconcern.org.uk

RICABILITY
30 Angel Gate
City Road
London EC1V 2PT
Tel: 020 7427 2460
Fax: 020 7427 2469
e-mail: mail@ricability.org.uk
Web: www.ricability.org.uk

THE PAIN RELIEF
FOUNDATION
Clinical Sciences Centre
University Hospital Aintree
Lower Lane
Liverpool L9 7AL
Tel: 0151 529 5820
Fax: 0151 529 5821
e-mail: secretary@painrelieffoundation.org.uk
Web: www.painrelieffoundation.org.uk

index

Photo Credits

Tony Hutchings, 32, 33, 34, 35, 36, 37
(Air Chair provided by Inova)
Mike King, 136
Getty Images, 46, 49, 50, 54, 57, 76, 78, 139, 144

PREVENTION Health Guides

Outsmart Arthritis

Reader Survey

Return this survey and you will be entered into a free prize draw to win one of two FREE one-year memberships to **fitness first**

Thank you for purchasing OUTSMART ARTHRITIS! We are very interested in finding out a little more about you so we can tailor future publications to your needs and interests. When you're finished, just tear out the survey and fax or mail it back to us:

Fax back to: **020 7291 6014**
Mail to: **Marketing Dept, Rodale Ltd, 7-10 Chandos Street, London W1G 9AD**

Thanks – we look forward to hearing from you!

WHAT DID YOU THINK?

1. Overall, how would you rate this publication: OUTSMART ARTHRITIS?
(Please tick one box)
❑ Excellent
❑ Very Good
❑ Good
❑ Fair
❑ Poor

2. Which of the following did you do prior to actually purchasing this publication? (Please tick all that apply)
❑ Looked at the cover
❑ Examined the contents page
❑ Skimmed several of the chapters
❑ Flipped through the whole publication
❑ Checked the price
❑ Compared it to other publications

3. Do you think the price you paid for this publication was:
(Please tick one box)
❑ Too high for the amount of information it contains
❑ Just right for the amount of information it contains
❑ Too low for the amount of information it contains

4. Which of the following cover lines made you want to buy this issue of OUTSMART ARTHRITIS?
(Please tick up to three choices)
❑ Stop The Pain And Feel Great
❑ Start this 30-day plan today!
❑ Take Control Of Your Life
❑ All your treatment options explained
❑ Eat To Beat Arthritis
❑ Delicious Recipes that Really Work
❑ Supplements - what to take and what to avoid
❑ How to walk and stretch away joint pain
❑ All new solutions for: Osteoarthritis, Rheumatoid Arthritis and Fibromyalgia

YOUR READING INTERESTS

5. Do you subscribe to any magazines?
❑ Yes
❑ No

6. If the answer is "yes", which magazines do you subscribe to?
(Please write in)
_____
_____
_____
_____

7. Do you buy any magazines from the shop?
❏ Yes
❏ No

8. If the answer is "yes", which magazines do you purchase?
(Please write in)
_____
_____
_____

9. Which of these condition-specific publications would interest you?
(Please tick up to three choices)
❏ Outsmart Allergies
❏ Outsmart Asthma
❏ Outsmart Cancer
❏ Outsmart Cholesterol
❏ Outsmart Disease: Complete A-to-Z Guide
❏ Outsmart Depression
❏ Outsmart Diabetes
❏ Outsmart Heart Disease
❏ Outsmart Your Hormones
❏ Outsmart Infertility
❏ Outsmart Osteoporosis
❏ Outsmart Menopause

ABOUT YOU

10. Are you?
❏ Male ❏ Female

11. What is your age? ____

12. What is your marital status?
(Please tick one box)
❏ Married
❏ Single
❏ Living with partner
❏ Separated, widowed, divorced

13. What is your occupation?
(Please tick one box)
❏ Professional/Senior manager
❏ Manager in Business
❏ Admin/Clerical
❏ Manual
❏ Housewife
❏ Student
❏ Retired
❏ Self Employed/Business Owner
❏ Other

14. What is your household income before taxes? (Please tick one box)
❏ Under £9,999
❏ £10,000 - £19,999
❏ £20,000 - £29,999
❏ £30,000 - £39,999
❏ £40,000 - £49,999
❏ £50,000 +

15. Any suggestions or comments?
_____
_____
_____
_____

Thank you for your help. Please complete your details below and return the completed survey to:

Marketing Dept, Rodale Ltd, 7-10 Chandos Street, London W1 9AD as soon as possible, or fax to 020 7291 6014.

All respondents will be entered into a free prize draw to win one of two free one-year memberships to Fitness First health club*.

Name: _____

Address: _____
_____
_____
Postcode: _____